A
BOOK
FOR
MUM

A BOOK FOR MUM

BECAUSE SHE'S SO SPECIAL

DIANA CRAIG

Michael O'Mara Books Limited

First published in Great Britain in 2011 by
Michael O'Mara Books Limited
9 Lion Yard
Tremadoc Road
London SW4 7NQ

Originally published in 2010 under the title *I Love You Mum*.

Copyright © Michael O'Mara Books Limited 2010, 2011

A CIP catalogue record for this book is available from the British
Library.

Papers used by Michael O'Mara Books Limited are natural,
recyclable products made from wood grown in sustainable forests.
The manufacturing processes conform to the environmental
regulations of the country of origin.

ISBN: 978-1-84317-665-7

1 2 3 4 5 6 7 8 9 10

www.mombooks.com

Designed and typeset by K DESIGN, Somerset

Printed and bound in Great Britain by Clays Ltd, St Ives plc

In memory of my mother

Contents

Introduction

Our mother's face is the first one we see when we enter the world. As babies, we are totally dependent on our mothers; a baby has only to cry and it will have its mum's attention. The sense of safety of those early days of infancy and toddlerhood stays with us forever. We seek it in our adult relationships. When we are ill, who do we want to tuck us up into bed and bring us soup and comfort? Mum. When we are scared, who do we want by our side, metaphorically holding our hand? Mum, again. With Mum to turn to, the world is safe. Our mothers always have a special place in our lives.

Of course, mums have different ways of relating to their children and this varies from one generation to the next. In earlier centuries, aristocratic mothers, or those from well-to-do families, had little contact with their offspring, who were handed over to wet nurses, nannies and governesses, and trotted out to see 'Mama' only at special times of day. In England, if you were a young boy from a wealthy family, you'd be shunted off to private boarding school at the tender age of seven – a practice that seems cruel to us now. In poorer families, it was the lot of the older children to look after their younger siblings.

It took a long time for things to change. A mere fifty or so years ago, 'experts' were advocating a strict regime for Baby lest he or she became spoilt by too much attention. Needless to say, these 'experts' were not mothers themselves or they would have known that to leave a baby crying goes against every maternal instinct. Imagine those poor women, desperately wanting to pick their baby up but restraining themselves because the book said they shouldn't. It's just not natural!

Modern mums have a more relaxed approach. Sometimes they make mistakes, but that's OK; they are human after all. Even when their kids drive them to distraction (and they will – ask any experienced mother), mums still want the best for their children and will do (almost) anything for them. That bond continues beyond babyhood, beyond toddlerhood, beyond adolescence and into adulthood. Once a mother, always a mother.

Being a mum is perhaps the most challenging – and most rewarding – job in the world. This book celebrates motherhood in all its glory and imperfection.

Out of the mouths ...

... of babes and sucklings. Indeed. This saying, of Biblical origin, means that pearls of wisdom often fall from the youngest lips. And one of an infant's first utterances is likely to be the name of the person who will do most to shape his or her world: 'mama'.

❧ First words ❧

Whatever culture they grow up in, a baby's first word is likely to be a variation of 'mama' – and there's a scientific reason for this. Although local names for 'mother' come from vastly different language groups and from very different parts of the world, they all sound similar. So what's going on here?

For years linguists were puzzled by this phenomenon. Various arguments were put forth, such as the suggestion that the words 'mama' and 'mummy' were the relics of some ancient proto-language from which all other tongues were descended. But the real explanation was obvious, and it was the famous Russian linguist Roman Osipovich Jakobson (1896–1982) who was among the first to spot it – by observing the way infants learn language.

The three stages

When it comes to getting verbal, kids are no slouches and learn their first language in progressive, orderly stages. Grammar and spelling can wait – their first challenge is to get their tongues around the sounds:

1. At first, an infant's only vocalizations are sobbing and shrieking (we all know about that!).
2. Next comes the 'cooing' stage, when the child makes those typical baby noises that don't resemble words.
3. Now for the exciting bit – for parents anyway. The third stage of vocalization is when an infant begins 'babbling' and experimenting with those sounds – vowels and consonants – that he or she will later combine to make words.

Say 'aah'

The easiest vowel sound is 'ah' because it requires no effort from the tongue or the lips. Just try it: open your mouth without forming your lips into any shape, make a noise and the sound that comes out will be 'ah'. (For vowels like 'oh' or 'ee', you have to move your lips.) So 'ah', because it's easiest, becomes a baby's earliest vowel sound.

But what about consonants? The labial consonants – the ones we form with our lips, such as 'm', 'b' and 'p' – are the simplest to produce because they require no work from the tongue; all you have to do is press your lips together momentarily. 'B' and 'p' are a tad more difficult, however, because they require the velum (the soft palate) at the back of the mouth to lift a little, which leaves 'm' as the clear front-runner. See where this is heading?

Armed with the easy 'm' and the easy 'ah', babies put these first two sounds together to form 'ma'. Or rather, 'ma-ma-ma-ma-ma' – nothing improves your linguistic skills more than babbling repetitiously in your pushchair.

Parents, of course, are quick to put their own interpretation on this as they crane to detect their child's first word. When they hear what sounds like 'mama' or 'mum', mothers are especially thrilled – little Susan or little Johnny is saying their name! In fact, babies typically make the 'ma-ma' sound as their first 'word' irrespective of their parents' language simply because it's easiest for them to vocalize.

Mamma mia!

Here are some variations on the theme:

- Ama – Basque
- Amma, Maa – Indian
- Amy – Kobon (New Guinea)

❁ Mama – Italian, Luo (Kenya), Mandarin, Quechua (Ecuador), Romanian, Spanish, Swahili

❁ Mam – Irish, Welsh

❁ Maman - French

❁ Mammy – Irish, American

❁ Mang – Urdu

❁ Mom, Mommy – American

❁ Mum, Mummy – Australian, British, Canadian, New Zealand

FOOD, GLORIOUS FOOD!

A baby's early babbled 'ma-ma's may also invite another interpretation. If Mother isn't the first thing on Baby's mind, what else could be? Well, what does a mother represent to her baby in the early days? A source of food! So 'mama' has also come to be the origin of the word for 'breast' in various languages, giving us *mamma* in Latin, *mama* in Hausa (Nigeria) and *-ama-* in Xhosa (South Africa)… and of course, from the Latin, mammal, mammalian, mammary gland, etc.

At mother's knee

Times have changed a lot since the days when stay-at-home mums were the norm and dads were the breadwinners and went out to work. But even now, when many young mothers choose – or have through financial necessity – to return to work after the birth of their babies, the bond between mother and infant remains a unique one.

❈ The hand that rocks the cradle ❈

Although many women still do not achieve the same status in the workplace as men, as mothers their influence can be enormous. The mother-child relationship is where it all begins; through the effect they have on their children, women can indirectly affect the world, as the American poet William Ross Wallace (1819–81) pointed out in his poem 'What Rules the World' with its famous two-line refrain, as in this verse:

Infancy's the tender fountain,
Power may with beauty flow,
Mother's first to guide the streamlets,
From them souls unresting grow –
Grow on for the good or evil,
Sunshine streamed or evil hurled;
For the hand that rocks the cradle
Is the hand that rules the world.

'The best academy, a mother's knee.'

JAMES RUSSELL LOWELL (1819–91)

❋ A good start ❋

Many a high-achiever has cited the importance of a mother – or mother figure – in giving them the foundation on which they were able to build their future success. Some began life poor with no obvious prospects or advantages – except, that is, for the benign influence of a maternal presence that was able to direct their destiny.

Richard Branson, multi-millionaire entrepreneur, writes in his inspiring and irresistibly titled little book *Screw It, Let's Do It* of the feisty, get-up-and-go atmosphere in which he grew up. When he was a child, his mother ran a business from home and all the kids did their part. He also recalls how she fostered his sense of independence when she made him, at the tender age of four, find his own way home across the fields (though most mothers now would undoubtedly shrink from going to such an extreme).

Barack Obama, who realized the hopes of many African-Americans and made history when he became the first Black president of the United States, was shaped by two generations of mothers. Writing of his own mother, Ann Dunham – traveller, civil rights activist and cultural anthropologist – he said: 'What is best in me, I owe to her.'

But it was his maternal grandmother, Madelyn Dunham, who was the most formative influence on his life. A native of no-nonsense Kansas, Madelyn later went to live in Hawaii, where she helped to raise the young Barack after his mother's marriage broke down. No mean achiever herself, Madelyn became one of the first women vice-presidents of the Bank of Hawaii, and instilled in her grandson her values of hard work, personal responsibility and self-reliance. 'She poured everything she had into me,' Obama later said of the woman he affectionately called Toot, from 'Tutu', the Hawaiian word for 'grandmother'.

Neither his mother nor his grandmother lived to see Obama become president. Ann died of ovarian cancer in 1995, aged just fifty-two; Madelyn passed away in 2008 at the age of eighty-six, on the eve of the presidential election.

Oprah Winfrey, mega media personality, publisher, film producer and actress, is further proof of the powerful influence a mother or mother figure can have in shaping a child's life. In Oprah's case, it was not her mother but her mother's mother who helped to sow the seeds of her destiny. Oprah was born in rural Mississippi, an illegitimate child. When her mother moved away, she left her own mother to care for the baby girl. Oprah later acknowledged how important her grandmother was in her development, describing how she taught her to read which opened doors that might otherwise have been closed and contributed to her future success.

❀ What they said ❀

Many other high-flyers have credited their mothers for their success. Here's what a few of them have to say:

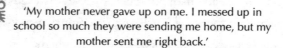

'My mother never gave up on me. I messed up in school so much they were sending me home, but my mother sent me right back.'

DENZEL WASHINGTON (1954–)

'My mother was the most beautiful woman I ever saw. All I am I owe to my mother. I attribute all my success in life to the moral, intellectual and physical education I received from her.'
GEORGE WASHINGTON (1732–99)

'*It seems to me that my mother was the most splendid woman I ever knew ... I have met a lot of people knocking around the world since, but I have never met a more thoroughly refined woman than my mother. If I have amounted to anything, it will be due to her.*'

CHARLIE CHAPLIN (1889–1977)

'I shall never forget my mother, for it was she who planted and nurtured the first seeds of good within me. She opened my heart to the lasting impressions of nature; she awakened my understanding and extended my horizon and her percepts exerted an everlasting influence upon the course of my life.'

IMMANUEL KANT (1724–1804)

'*Fifty-four years of love and tenderness and crossness and devotion and unswerving loyalty. Without her I could have achieved a quarter of what I have achieved, not only in terms of success and career, but in terms of personal happiness ... She has never stood between me and my life, never tried to hold me too tightly, always let me go free ...*'

NÖEL COWARD (1899–1973)

'*The future destiny of the child is always the work of the mother.*'

NAPOLEON BONAPARTE (1769–1821)

'My mother was the making of me. She was so true
and so sure of me, I felt that I had someone to live for –
someone I must not disappoint. The memory of my
mother will always be a blessing to me.'

THOMAS EDISON (1847–1931)

IN A WORD

If you are in any doubt about the crucial role of
mothers, just look at the high regard they are given
in our language, which sees 'mother' as the source
from which all things spring:

※ Mother church – a principal church from
which others have originated

※ Mother country/motherland – one's homeland
or native land

※ Mother Earth – the personification of the earth
on which life itself depends – the message
doesn't get stonger than this. The ancient
Greeks made Mother Earth into a goddess and
called her Gaia

※ Mother ship – a vessel in charge of smaller craft

※ Mother tongue – one's first language

※ Mother wit – inborn common sense

'*The doctors told me that I would never walk, but my mother told me I would, so I believed my mother.*'
WILMA RUDOLPH, ATHLETE (1940–94)

'*Mama exhorted her children at every opportunity to "jump at de sun".We might not land on the sun, but at least we would get off the ground.*'
ZORA NEALE HURSTON, ANTHROPOLOGIST (1903–60)

A womb of her own

'It takes two to get one into trouble,' quipped Mae West. Whatever a woman feels about the news that she is pregnant, bearing a child is her rite of passage into a totally new phase of her life: motherhood. With the arrival of children, nothing is ever the same again.

> 'The solution to adult problems tomorrow depends in large measure upon how our children grow up today.'
>
> MARGARET MEAD (1901–1978)

Single mothers

Some mothers – those with connections in high places – are able to bypass the whole messy conception process and do it pretty much alone, becoming mothers with barely a man in sight. The Greeks had a swanky word for it: *parthenogenesis*, literally 'virgin birth'. You go girl!

Coatlicue, the Aztec mother goddess and patron of women who die in childbirth was doing a spot of housework one day when a ball of feathers fell down from above and touched her and – hey presto! – she was instantly pregnant. That's what she said, anyway, but the story didn't wash with the many children she already had, and they decided to kill her for being such a hussy. Luckily for Coatlicue, her son Huitzilopochtli (aka the Blue Hummingbird), god of the sun and war, sprang from her body and dispatched the lot of them.

The Virgin Mary is perhaps the most famous woman to have circumvented the entire conception stage and become pregnant while still a virgin – and while unmarried to boot. Given her situation, Mary was understandably extremely surprised when the Angel Gabriel announced the good news to her.

Danaë caught the eye of the Greek father god Zeus (maidens were always catching his eye). However, Danaë's father had heard a prediction that his grandson would one day kill him. Determined that his daughter should not have a child, he shut her up in a tower to keep the men away. But he had reckoned without Zeus, who simply transformed himself into a shower of golden rain and drifted in through Danae's window. The result? The hero Perseus, who went on to kill the Medusa.

Dechtire, an Irish goddess, swallowed a may fly and became pregnant with the hero Cuchulainn – which gives a new slant to the lyrics of the song: 'There was an old woman who swallowed a fly, I don't know why she swallowed a fly...'

'Death and taxes and childbirth! There's never a convenient time for any of them.'

MARGARET MITCHELL (1900–1949)

❧ Caught short ❧

Some mums give birth in hospital, some at home and some ... well, take a look at the following venues:

❀ A woman in Mozambique gave birth in the tree in which she found herself stranded during a flood. 'Rock-a-bye baby on the treetop' seems an appropriate lullaby.

❀ An American college student didn't even realize she was pregnant, and spent twelve hours in labour in her dormitory believing she was just having bad cramps.

❀ A mother in Cambridge went into labour while topping up her mobile phone in the local post office. Before the ambulance could arrive, she delivered a healthy baby girl weighing in at just under 2.7kg (6lb)

– luckily the postmaster was there to check on this with his scales.

❁ In 2009, Julia Kowalska was on London Underground's Jubilee Line when her contractions started. She got off at Kingsbury station and realized she was in labour. An ambulance was called but the crew decided there wasn't enough time to get her to hospital and, thirty-five minutes later, she gave birth to a baby girl in the station supervisor's office.

❁ In Fullerton, California, a woman was caught short on her way home from shopping, with her two-year-old asleep in the back of the car. She went into labour – six weeks before her due date – and gave birth on her front lawn.

❁ During the German bombing of London in World War II, the Underground provided shelter for the city's inhabitants. But babies don't know anything about air raid restrictions and arrive when they want to. Of the babies who were born on the Underground during the war, one of the most famous is Jerry Springer, who claims to have made his debut at East Finchley station in North London in 1944.

'I stood in the hospital corridor the night after she was born. Through a window I could see all the small, crying newborn infants, and somewhere among them slept the one who was mine. I stood there for hours filled with happiness until the night nurse sent me to bed.'

LIV ULLMAN (1938–)

A PIECE OF CAKE

In the 1983 Monty Python film *The Meaning of Life*, a weary pregnant woman, played by Eric Idle, stands by a kitchen sink when a baby, complete with umbilical cord, plops out onto the floor between her legs. Without batting an eye, she turns to her daughter and says: 'Get that, will you, Deirdre?'

✸ What's age got to do with it? ✸

Although there have been reports of girls giving birth at an extremely young age, the trend – in the developed Western world at least – is for women to postpone motherhood. Doctors warn that the optimum age for having babies is still in the 20–35 age bracket, but some women are delaying motherhood until their forties. Of course, good prenatal care and modern obstetrics make it more possible to have a healthy birth, while fertility treatments can bring hope to those who desperately want children but have difficulty conceiving.

> 'Somewhere on this globe, every ten seconds, there is a woman giving birth to a child. She must be found and stopped.'
>
> SAM LEVENSON (1911–80)

T'was ever thus ...

When it comes to late-life births, nothing can match what goes on in the Bible. In the Old Testament, Sarah, wife of the patriarch Abraham, was a sprightly ninety years – and her husband hitting 100 – when she overheard three visitors talking to him in his tent. The three were, of course, angels of the Lord in disguise. They told Abraham that Sarah – barren for years and 'well stricken in age' – would bear him a son. Sarah laughed at such a ridiculous proposition for, after all, 'it had ceased to be with her after the manner of women'. 'After I am waxed old shall I have pleasure, my lord being old also?' she asks herself cynically – the days of any kind of hanky-panky are long gone. God notices her disrespectful attitude and challenges Abraham as to his wife's behaviour. 'I didn't laugh,' lies Sarah. 'Oh yes, you did,' insists God. Of course, God is right and Sarah is wrong, and in due course she does indeed give birth to a son: Isaac.

Elizabeth, cousin of the Virgin Mary, and her husband Zachariah were also 'well stricken in years' when the angel Gabriel came to announce the forthcoming event: that she would give birth to John the Baptist.

> 'There is nothing more thrilling in this world, I think, than having a child that is yours, and yet is mysteriously a stranger.'
>
> AGATHA CHRISTIE (1890–1976)

❧ Latecomers ❧

❀ In Italy in 1994, fertility treatment made it possible for Rosanna Dalla Corte to give birth to a baby boy – at the age of sixty-three.

❀ In Britain in 2008, IVF treatment paid for in Russia enabled Susan Tollefsen to have her first child – a daughter called Freya – at the age of fifty-seven.

❀ In Spain in 2006 Maria Carmen del Bousada gave birth to twins days before her sixty-seventh birthday, making her the world's oldest mum.

Bringing up baby

It's not easy being a mum – especially if it's a woman's first time. The advice flies – from friends, mothers and, yes, mothers-in-law. The way your mother parented you may have been as much down to the parenting style prevalent at the time as to her personal preferences.

❋ Tough love ❋

Attitudes to childrearing have changed enormously over the centuries, with different experts pontificating to mothers on the 'right' way to bring up their children. A disciplinarian approach was long favoured for fear that too much kindness would turn a child into a spoilt brat. Forget a no-smacking policy (mothers still disagree about this one) – just take a look at these nifty pieces of advice from earlier centuries:

❋ He that spareth the rode, hates the childe.

❋ A good rodde make a good boy.

❋   A child may have too much of his mother's blessing.

The Duchess in *Alice in Wonderland* was of the same mind:

> *Speak roughly to your little boy,*
>   *And beat him when he sneezes:*
> *He only does it to annoy,*
>   *Because he knows it teases.*
> *I speak severely to my boy,*
>   *I beat him when he sneezes;*
> *For he can thoroughly enjoy*
>   *The pepper when he pleases!*

❋ No mollycoddling! ❋

Mums, if you want your child to grow up into a well-balanced, fully rounded adult, forget all that soppy huggling and cuddling and 'kissing it better'. Everything you need to know is contained in the pages of *Psychological Care of Infant and Child*, written by the American psychologist John Broadus Watson (1878–1958) and published in 1928:

'Nearly all of us have suffered from over-coddling in our infancy. How does it show? It shows in invalidism … coddling is a dangerous experiment … the fact that our children are always crying and always whining shows the unhappy, unwholesome state they are in. There is a sensible way of treating children. Treat them as though they were young adults. Never hug and kiss them, never let them sit on your lap. If you must, kiss them once on the forehead when they say good night. Shake hands with them in the morning … try it out. In a week's time you will be utterly ashamed of the mawkish, sentimental way you have been handling it …'

So now you know.

❦ Many hands ❦

In earlier times when broods were bigger, the older children – especially the girls – would be set the task of deputizing as 'little mothers' and caring for their younger siblings. In doing so, they learnt useful mothering skills that they could later apply to their own children; and for their hard-pressed mothers there was no other practical solution. Spare a thought, though, for a Mrs Vassilyev of Russia who, between 1725 and 1765, is said to have produced sixty-nine children. Or the mother of the English artist and writer Edward Lear (1812–88), who had a modest twenty-one offspring. Perhaps, when pressed, they resorted to the same tactic as the Old Woman of nursery-rhyme fame:

> *There was an old woman who lived in a shoe,*
> *She had so many children she didn't know what to do;*
> *She gave them some broth without any bread;*
> *She whipped them all soundly and put them to bed.*

The old woman in this well-known rhyme has been identified with, among others, Caroline, wife of King George II, who had eight children; and Elizabeth Vergoose who lived in Boston in the United States, and had six children of her own and ten stepchildren. Just imagine what it must have been like when they all sat down to eat!

❧ Look no further … ❧

The twentieth century saw the publication of a number of childcare manuals that influenced the way in which whole generations of mothers brought up their children. The watershed between the different parenting styles seems to have been World War II.

The fifties mum

Mothers in the 1950s were still hugely influenced by the no-nonsense approach of Sir Frederick Truby King, who had published his *Feeding and Care of Babies* back in 1907. Originally based in New Zealand, Truby King later practised as a surgeon in Scotland. Like John Watson (see page 30), he was very much of the 'tough-love' school. Although he advocated breastfeeding, he was a firm believer in discipline right from the word go, and advised mothers to:

❃   put their babies in a separate room from the beginning

❃   feed them by the clock every four hours and never at night

❋ resist giving in to tears and let them 'cry it out' – babies had to learn that they couldn't always get what they wanted

❋ leave them to sleep between feeds

❋ put them outside on their own during the day as much as possible – fresh air would toughen them up

❋ avoid cuddling or comforting them

❋ avoid playing with them too much – play would only over-excite them

Fathers had no role to play, other than as breadwinners, in Truby King's universe. All this was designed to be character-building; it may have produced grown men with the classic British stiff upper lip – the backbone of Empire – but who knows what unhappiness lurked beneath those impassive exteriors.

The sixties mum

It was all change in the Swinging Sixties. The definitive influence now was a multi-million bestseller called *The Common Sense Book of Baby and Child Care* which had been published in 1946 and written by a Dr Spock – no, not the funny guy with the pointy ears from Star Trek, but an American pediatrician whose first name was Benjamin.

Spock's approach couldn't have been further from that of Truby King. You'll get loads of conflicting advice, he warned young mothers, but trust your instincts as to what your baby needs: 'You know more than you think you do.' Feed your child on demand, pick him up whenever he cries, play with her as much as you like, let him sleep in your bed ... The difference was seismic.

The famous American anthropologist Margaret Mead was one of the first mothers to follow the Spock method, at a time before he came to fame and was still a largely unknown pediatrician. Mead had lived in Samoa and studied the culture there, and Spock's innovative approach to childrearing chimed with her own views. After her daughter Mary Catherine was born in 1939, the doctor encouraged her to breastfeed her on demand, a practice that was not widely accepted in the US medical community then. Today, it seems extraordinary to us that anyone should doubt such an approach – it is, after all, just 'common sense' and the most natural thing in the world.

English psychiatrist John Bowlby was with Dr Spock on this when he developed his ideas on 'attachment theory' – the importance of the bond between child and mother. In 1953, Bowlby published his bestseller *Child Care and the Growth of Love*. When mums paid attention to their babies in a myriad of little intimate ways, he said – cuddling and playing with them, breastfeeding, washing and dressing them – they were laying the foundations for their child's sense of self worth; none of that 'leave a baby to cry in the cot' nonsense for Bowlby. Unfortunately, his theories backfired slightly when mothers starting feeling guilty for returning to work, worrying that they might be damaging their children by their absence.

'Nobody has ever before asked the nuclear family to live all by itself in a box the way we do. With no relatives, no support, we've put it in an impossible situation.'

MARGARET MEAD (1901–78)

The seventies mum

By the seventies, mothering was getting even more touchy-feely. One approach was that advocated by American anthropologist Jean Liedloff in her 1975 book *The Continuum Concept*. Like Margaret Mead, Liedloff had spent time with so-called 'primitive' peoples, in this case two years with South American Indians. Observing how much close physical contact their children received and how happy and well-balanced they were, she advocated that babies should have continual skin-to-skin contact for at least the first year of life. The way to do this was to carry them around in a sling while you got on with your day, and let them sleep in your bed at night. (Those groans you hear are Truby King turning in his grave ...)

Three years later another bestselling childcare manual hit the shelves: *Your Baby and Child: From Birth to Age Five* by British psychologist and parenting guru Penelope Leach. Exploring what happens at each of the developmental stages in the first five years of life, it advised mothers to be guided by their children and also to listen to their own feelings. It was a circular loop: the happier you could make your baby, the happier you would be.

Teatime temptations

Everything stops for tea and, whatever the occasion, the teatime table needs tempting snacks. As always, it's presentation that matters.

❊ Make it fun! ❊

Size matters too; kids find smaller, daintier shapes more appealing and if they resemble some recognizable object – say a face or an animal – they like them even more. The following ideas are so simple that you might get your children to help make them.

Sandwich shapes

Make sandwiches from thin slices of bread and fill with peanut butter, egg mayonnaise or some other fairly smooth filling. Use fancy pastry cutters to cut them into different shapes, such as animals or gingerbread men.

Yellow hedgehog

The old favourite! Cut a large grapefuit in half and attach raisin eyes and a nose to it with little blobs of cream cheese. Put some small cubes of cheese and pineapple on cocktail sticks, then insert the sticks into the grapefruit half for the hedgehog's spines.

Jewel biscuits

This is a relic from birthday parties of my own childhood. With a child's love of colour and decoration, I adored these jewel-like biscuits – it wasn't the taste that mattered so much as the look. Mums will be relieved to know that they are easy to make – and cheap! Just butter some rich tea biscuits and sprinkle with hundreds and thousands for an instant party treat.

Biscuit faces

Pipe faces onto some plain biscuits, such as digestives, with cream cheese or buttercream icing. Add raisins for eyes and half a chocolate button for a nose.

❦ Let them eat cake! ❦

At birthday time, the cake is the centrepiece of the table, but children's novelty birthday cakes can cost a fortune, especially if you go for a 'bespoke' designer cake. But you don't have to spend vast amounts of money; you can make your own novelty cakes without too much trouble and with a lot of fun. All you need are some ready-made ingredients and your own creative Inner Child to help put them all together.

When my daughters were little, I remember slaving away to make fancy birthday cakes. On one occasion, I'd decided on a Hansel and Gretel house. I baked two loaf sponges to make the house and roof. I then spent hours decorating it to match what I thought was every child's fantasy of a magical gingerbread house. Did the birthday girl and her guests appreciate my efforts? Maybe. But what they seemed to like most were the Smarties decorating the roof – they picked off and ate every one – and left the cake.

Such was my sense of maternal responsibility that, for another birthday party, I made homemade chocolate ice cream. From scratch. Did the kids notice the depth of flavour of the fairtrade organic chocolate (70 per cent cocoa solids, naturally)? Or the richness of the free-range, organic eggs and the organic cream? I doubt it. They would have been just as happy with a decent ice cream from the supermarket.

The lesson here is: for children's parties, presentation is all. It's not the content but the bling – all those sparkly bits, those multicoloured decorations – that counts with kids. Wise mums have learnt that they don't need to be *Cordon Bleu* cooks to put on a good spread for a birthday – they just need some time and imagination.

Be creative!

Easy novelty cake-making begins with two basic shapes: cylinders and cubes. Cakes in these shapes can be bought ready-made from the baker's or supermarket, but it's what a creative mum does with them that transforms them into something special. Here are some useful items in the creative cake-maker's armoury ...

❈ wafer biscuits – their criss-cross texture makes them excellent roof tiles

❈ round biscuits, for the wheels of trains or cars

❈ icing flowers (the kind sold along with the hundreds and thousands), for 'gardens'

❈ small sweets (Dolly Mixtures, mini-fruit pastilles, Smarties, silver balls, etc), for 'jewels'

❈ foil-wrapped chocolate coins, for pirate's treasure

❈ drinking straws (stripey, if possible), for ship's masts

And not forgetting the one essential ingredient:

❈ buttercream icing: this is the confectioner's 'glue' that sticks one part to another, and that covers the finished cakes to obscure the joins (it can be coloured with food colouring, as necessary)

Take one Swiss roll ...

It's amazing what you can do with a Swiss roll!

❀ **Choo-choo train**

A large Swiss roll and, say, four mini-rolls, arranged in a line, make a great steam engine and carriages. Another mini-roll, cut in half, will do for the chimney, round biscuits (such as jammie dodgers) for the wheels, and wafer biscuits for the bumper in front of the engine – all glued together, of course, with buttercream icing. Committed trainspotters may feel that the detail falls short of the real thing – in which case, mums can check out photographs of steam trains and use small fairy cakes or marshmallows for the other lumps and bumps that make up the engine's silhouette.

❀ **Creepy caterpillar**

Small boys, with their fascination for creepy crawlies, may like this best, and it couldn't be easier to put together. Depending on the shape and size required, two or three Swiss rolls – arranged in a line as for the train – can make up the body, with two Liquorice Allsort slices for eyes.

❀ **Windmill or rocket**

An upended Swiss roll, with an ice cream cone on top for the roof, becomes a windmill or a rocket.

Triangular ice cream wafers, cut to shape, can make the fins at the base of the rocket, while wafer biscuits could do for the windmill's sails. Or, with a bit of adaptation, this could become Rapunzel's tower.

Take one Madeira cake ...

A rectangular loaf-shaped sponge is a great basic shape for a number of inventive novelty cakes. Madeira cake is especially good; not only does it taste delicious, but its firm texture makes it easy to cut to shape.

✻ **Treasure chest**

This is such an easy cake to put together. It's based on two Madeira cakes – one whole one for the body of the chest and a thick slice of the other for the lid. Liquorice strips make convincing iron bands to go around the chest. The fun bit is arranging the 'treasure' that should spill out from inside – chocolate coins, candy necklaces, mini-sweets, etc. The lid can then be propped on top.

✻ **Hansel and Gretel's cottage**

Another easy one – one Madeira cake for the main part of the house and a second one, sliced in half diagonally, popped on top for the roof. A mini-Swiss roll would do for the chimney. In the fairy story, the witch's house was made of gingerbread and candy – a child's dream – so it's impossible to go over the top in decorating this cake. It should positively sparkle with sugary confections. Pink wafer biscuits or rows of Smarties make a good roof covering, while suitable biscuits work well for the door and windows.

❋ Noah's Ark

With a bit of adaptation – and the addition of some animal-shaped biscuits (which can be found in the supermarket) – Hansel and Gretel's cottage can become Noah's Ark.

Mix 'n' match

Is there no end to the creative fun? By combining cubes (Madeira cakes) with cylinders (Swiss rolls), a mum can produce her *pièce de resistance* – a magical Cinderella's castle. Two Madeira cakes, cut in half, make four castle walls. A full-sized Swiss roll, topped with an ice-cream-cone 'roof' can make an inner tower, while mini-rolls will work as turrets. Striped drinking straws can make flag poles, attached to greaseproof paper 'flags'.

Alternatively, a whole, upended Madeira cake, surrounded by towers and turrets of different sizes and heights, makes for a more Disney-esque castle.

❀ **The best sleepover ever** ❀

So you've finally given in and allowed your child to have a sleepover as part of a birthday party. Unbeknownst to your child, who will expect you to make yourself scarce for the whole night and pretend you can't hear the sounds of midnight feasts and computer games, your behind-the-scenes presence and preparation are what will make the party flow from one fun activity to the next.

There are two golden rules when it comes to hosting the perfect sleepover, which will guarantee that your child's party has the edge over everyone else's.

1. **Your child is in charge**

   Or so he or she must think: meddling mums are no fun at sleepovers.

   ❀ Ask your child in advance to help you plan what to serve for supper and breakfast, picking and choosing from their suggestions the things that you planned to make all along

   ❀ Buy or rent a selection of pre-approved movies and tell the kids they can watch whichever ones they want

   ❀ Plan how a computer-game championship might easily be organized, working out how many people ought to be in each team and how points systems might work, and get your child to suggest it to the group

2. **Relax the rules**

Children think that two sleepovers must-haves are a midnight feast and a scary movie, so you'll need to come up with a way to let them have their fun without compromising your sanity.

❊ In preparation for a raid on the kitchen, try to have some decent snacks 'lying around', but avoid anything too sugary or caffeinated if you plan on getting any sleep, or anything in breakable containers that might require urgent clearing-up in the early hours of the morning

❊ Do a bit of research to source movies that have just the right level of suspense/action for your child's age group, so that the kids get to watch something exciting but don't go home traumatized

❊ Accept that there will be chatter throughout the night and only make an appearance in your nightie if the noise becomes unacceptable or is keeping everyone awake

Pimples, peers and puberty

If there's one thing that never changes about the job of mothering, it's that it's always changing; every stage is a new experience, requiring different skills. Just when a mother thinks she's got the hang of it, along come puberty, pimples and peer pressure – her children have morphed into teenagers. Even the most grounded mum may sometimes find it hard to keep her temper – and her sanity – during her children's adolescence.

❦ The nature of the beast ❦

In a way, the 'terrible teens' are a repetition of the 'terrible twos', as youngsters begin the journey into adulthood and seek to assert their independence from their parents. Like boats released from their moorings, teenagers have discovered a new power: they don't have to listen to their parents any more. Too big to pick up and plop back in their buggies, they can simply walk away while mum or dad are talking. So, if your mum was less than perfect during your teen years, give her a break: she was dealing with an alien species – an adolescent.

'Adolescence is a period of rapid changes.
Between the ages of twelve and seventeen, for example,
a parent ages as much as twenty years.'

ANONYMOUS

❄ What mothers have to deal with ❄

❄ Teenagers are big – in fact, they may well be bigger and stronger than their parents. 'Go to your room,' doesn't work with a six-foot-tall teenage son.

❄ Teenagers have a strong sense of (in)justice. 'It's not *faaair!*' is a popular, knee-jerk response in many situations.

❄ Teenagers are bored. 'Yeah, whatever,' is a handy phrase that can be trotted out in answer to most parental statements and requests.

❄ Teenagers have Friends. A teenager's peer group can exert huge influence on how they dress and behave. Although adolescents like to pretend to be independent, in actual fact they want to be the same as everyone else.

❅ Teenagers are expensive to run. It may sometimes seem as if they have holes in their pockets. Where does it all go? To pay for all those things they need to keep in with their peer group, of course.

❅ Teenagers are deaf. Or so you might think from the volume of the music.

❅ Teenagers are oblivious. So it's one in the morning and they aren't home? What's the problem? The club didn't open till eleven. Chill.

❅ Teenagers are like Dracula. They sleep by day and become active at night.

❅ Teenagers speak a foreign language. They start to talk in street slang, or even in a different accent. Using street slang greatly enhances your cool.

❅ Teenagers are accomplished liars. 'But so-and-so's mother allows them to,' they insist smoothly, when arguing about staying out late/going to clubs, etc. Wise mothers know to check this out.

❅ Teenagers are embarrassed by their parents. Too close an association with your parents does not enhance your cool. They may walk several feet away from them when out together in public.

'A suburban mother's role is to deliver children obstetrically once, and by car forever after.'

PETER DE VRIES (1910–93)

❄ **What teenagers face** ❄

Yes, it's difficult being a mother of a teenager, but perceptive mothers realize that adolescent behaviour is often due to underlying insecurities. The teens are, after all, a time of enormous change. Adolescents have to deal with: puberty and becoming sexual beings; important exams that could influence the course of their lives; peer group pressure.

Underneath all that bravado and apparent confidence are youngsters who are deeply unsure of themselves and need their mums more than ever.

'What do girls do who haven't any mothers to help them through their troubles?'

LOUISA MAY ALCOTT (1832–88)

DON'T DO IT!

Nose studs, messy hair, jeans with the crotch halfway down their legs – these are just some of the ways teenagers signal their streetwise status and show that they aren't bound by those boring old conventions their parents follow. The truth is, they would die of embarrassment if their parents did behave in unconventional ways. Dads are especially prone to this, but mums aren't blameless either. Mums (and dads) can embarrass their teenage children if they:

* act or dress younger (or sexier) than their age. Unless a mum has a fabulous figure, mini-skirts and cleavages are no-nos (and even if she does have a fabulous figure, it's probably still a no-no). For dads, this means no tight jeans – there's nothing more unattractive than a belly overhang. Many middle-aged men don't know this.

* try to act cool or use street slang. No one is fooled.

* swear or drink too much in front of their teenager and their friends.

* show baby pictures of their teenager to their friends.

※ make jokes about sex or kiss their partner in front of their teenager. This is a hint that they just might have a sex life. Yuck. That is just so, like, gross!

It's simple really. All that adolescent children want is for their parents to blend into the background but keep their purse open at all times.

'Blaming mother is just another way of clinging to her still.'

NANCY FRIDAY (1933–)

The empty nest

You spend years bringing them up, preparing them for the time when they will – hopefully – become responsible, independent young adults. And then suddenly, one day, it happens. Mission Accomplished. The kids are 'grown-up' enough to leave home. All mums go through this at some point, and it's an experience that is not without sadness. Her fledgings are leaving the nest, which is why it's known as the Empty Nest Syndrome.

✼ Going, going, gone ✼

Think about it – a mother may spend as much as eighteen years caring for a child. Even if she is working, much of her time will revolve around the family. A mum's 'job' is a mixture of nurse and teacher. In the early days, it involves simple things like ensuring her child eats properly and teaching him/her important life skills and more straight-forward things such as how to tell the time and how to tie shoelaces. Later, it might be teaching her teenager how to drive. Being a mother is an all-consuming job, so when the kids leave home, all those old responsibilities go with them. No wonder a mother might feel at a loss! A large part of her identity has just walked out the door.

> 'The best way to keep children home is to make the home atmosphere pleasant – and let the air out of the tyres.'
>
> DOROTHY PARKER (1893–1967)

✤ What wise mums know ✤

Preparing your child for adulthood means gradually teaching them the skills they will need when they are out in the world on their own. Cooking all their meals for them, picking up after them and just being a general skivvy may seem like acts of loving sacrifice. In fact, doing this short-changes them; a child with no practical skills will leave home ill-equipped for life.

It will all come out in the wash

As soon as they are old enough, wise mums teach their children how to use the washing machine. They resist the temptation to do their children's washing for them – and refuse to be drawn into the washerwoman role when the kids return home from university for the holidays, lugging mountains of dirty items with them. This applies especially to sons who seem to develop a sudden and strange incapacity when the words 'washing machine' are mentioned. Remember, mums, that your son will one day be some other woman's husband. So show him how to use the washing machine and give your future daughter-in-law a break!

One smart parent got over washing machine phobia with this cunning ploy. She explained to her child that, if he wanted to learn to drive, he should first practise on the washing machine. A car is a machine too, she reasoned, so if he learned how to handle this one, it would improve his chances of being able to handle the other. But for this strategy to work, you need to catch 'em young ...

'There isn't a child who hasn't gone out into the brave new world who eventually doesn't return to the old homestead carrying a bundle of dirty clothes.'

ART BUCHWALD (1925–2007)

❄ Make the change ❄

The phase between being a dependent living at home and living independently away from home is a particularly challenging time in the mother-child relationship. Wise mums know that the rules are changing.

Visiting hours

When visiting her child in their student room or flat at university, a wise mum doesn't cast silent glances around the space, wrinkle her nose as if she has just smelt a decaying corpse or ask her child if they have a vacuum cleaner. She can smell the damp in the walls and knows that the place probably needs an industrial clean, but this is her offspring's new nest and they either aren't bothered by the mess, or are proud of their creative efforts to make it their own. Wise mums know to let go lightly – and her fledglings will more readily fly back to her.

Keep it to yourself

When the kids come home from college for the holidays, they bring their own routines with them. These may be just as irritating as their old routines but the rules are different now. Yes, it is irksome to be leaving to catch a crowded 7.30 train to work when your offspring are still oblivious under a warm duvet – and no doubt will be for several hours yet – but wise mums know to allow them their brief illusion of freedom. Their time will come ...

'It will be gone before you know it.
The fingerprints on the wall appear higher and higher.
Then suddenly they disappear.'

DOROTHY EVSLIN

❧ **Treasure the moment** ❧

No matter how much they drive her mad, a wise mum always reminds herself that one day her young will fly the nest – so she treasures them even more while she still has them. She knows they will be gone in the flash of a wing.

> 'There came a moment quite suddenly a mother realized that a child was no longer hers ... without bothering to ask or even give notice, her daughter had just grown up.'
>
> ALICE HOFFMAN (1952–)

❧ **I'll be back!** ❧

The trick, of course, to surviving the empty nest is for mums to have interests and ambitions of their own, outside of being a mother. Then, when the kids do go, it won't be quite so devastating. There's comfort to be gained, too, from the knowledge that the empty nest won't be empty forever. When the kids decide that that university course isn't for them, when they can't get a job and are broke, when they can't afford a mortgage, when they split up with their partner, they'll return – like well-trained homing pigeons – to take up snug residence under the old parental roof once more. The 'boomerang children' are back ...

'You see much more of your children once
they leave home.'

LUCILLE BALL (1911–89)

Just like my mother

It happens to all of us women. One day, we are going along perfectly happily being our fabulous individual selves. The next day, we look in the mirror and what do we see? Our mother, staring back at us. Looking like our mothers seems to increase with age, but the insidious trend can start even earlier, with the way we sound. Do you remember when you were still living at home and the phone rang – and the person at the other end of the line mistook you for your mum? Somehow, somewhere along the line, we seem to become clones of the woman who gave us birth.

'Your son is your son till he gets him a wife; your daughter's your daughter for all of your life.'

ANONYMOUS

❀ In Mother's footsteps ❀

As well as looking like them physically, many daughters follow in their mothers' footsteps in terms of career. Here are some of the more famous ones:

❀ Christabel and Sylvia Pankhurst, British suffragists and daughters of British suffragist Emmeline Pankhurst

❀ Emma Thompson, actress and daughter of actress Phyllida Law

❀ Gwyneth Paltrow, actress and daughter of actress Blythe Danner

❀ Kate Hudson, actress and daughter of actress Goldie Hawn

❀ Irène Joliot-Curie, scientist and Nobel Prizewinner, and daughter of scientist and Nobel Prizewinner Marie Curie

❀ Isabella Rossellini, actress, model, filmmaker and author, and daughter of actress Ingrid Bergman

❀ Keira Knightley, actress and daughter of actress-turned-playwright Sharman Macdonald

❀ Kelly Osbourne, celebrity and daughter of celebrity Sharon Osbourne

* Liza Minelli, singer and daughter of singer Judy Garland

* Shirley Williams, British politician and daughter of feminist and author Vera Brittain

* Mary Shelley, author of *Frankenstein* and daughter of Mary Wollstonecraft, author and eighteenth-century radical feminist

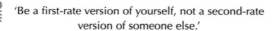

'Be a first-rate version of yourself, not a second-rate version of someone else.'

JUDY GARLAND (1922–69) TO HER DAUGHTER, LIZA MINELLI

Let me kiss it better

No matter how old we are, memories of being looked after by our mother when we were sick never fade. She tucked us up in bed, brought us soup or toast to eat, treated us with simple remedies and sat by our bedside to read us stories or stroke our hair. It was her love and concern that contributed to our recovery perhaps as much as the medications that were used. She made us feel safe. When we are ill, who wouldn't want to tucked up in bed by Mum?

✲ Mum – the best medicine ✲

The remedies our mothers used go back generations in some cases – old-fashioned treatments handed down from mother to daughter and used to relieve common ailments from colds, sore throats and fevers to tummy upsets, stings and grazes.

For blocked noses

❋ Rub patient's chest and back with a menthol rub.

❋ At bedtime, sprinkle eucalyptus oil on the pillow so the patient will breathe it in during sleep.

❋ Prepare a bowl of steaming water containing a few drops of methol rub or eucalyptus oil, cover patient's head with a towel and get the patient to bend over the bowl and breathe in the menthol vapour.

For all infections

❋ Tuck patient up in warm, cosy bed.

❋ Visit often, to soothe and comfort.

❋ Read bedtime stories, to lull patient to sleep.

For sore throats and coughs

❋ Dilute salt in warm water and have the patient use the solution as a gargle.

❋ Offer the patient a spoonful of honey diluted in a cup of warm water; or, if the patient is older, offer a hot toddy (warmed water containing whisky, lemon and honey).

For fever

❋ Give the patient plenty of water and juice to replace lost fluids.

❋ Take the temperature regularly and give medication to reduce fever.

❋ Apply a cold flannel to the forehead to cool the patient down.

For toothache and mouth ulcers

❋ Apply a drop of oil of cloves to a wad of cotton wool and hold against the affected site.

❋ Hold a cube of ice against the aching tooth.

❋ For mouth ulcers and small infections that may cause toothache, give the patient a salt-water mouthwash to gargle with. Stay with younger patients while they do this to ensure that they do not swallow the solution.

For splinters

❋ Grip end of splinter with pair of sterilized tweezers and extract, in same direction as splinter went in.

❋ For more embedded splinters, make a small incision in skin with a fine needle (sterilized over a flame or in boiling water) to expose the head. Very gently introduce the needle under the head of the splinter to allow tweezers to grip it and pull the splinter out.

❋ Soak the affected area in warm, soapy water, ideally in the bath, and the splinter should slide out.

For upset tummies

❋ Give the patient sweetened ginger or mint tea.

❋ Give the patient flat ginger ale or cola.

For cuts and grazes

❋ Kiss it better.

❋ Apply antiseptic ointment.

For sunburn

❋ Apply cool, used teabags to the skin.

❋ Apply cucumber slices to the skin.

❋ Dab honey onto the sunburnt area.

❋ Dab calamine lotion onto the sunburnt area.

For burns

❋ Immerse the burnt area in cool water – but don't apply ice to it!

For bee stings

❊ Talk to the patient and give plenty of cuddles to reassure them and distract them from the pain.

❊ Apply ice to the sting area, it will reduce any swelling and help to numb the pain.

❊ You could try a dab of toothpaste – apparently it works a treat!

For tears

❊ Give patient lots of cuddles.

❊ After a visit to the doctor or dentist, promise a small reward. A special outing, a little toy or favourite TV show should do the trick.

'My mother taught me to walk proud and tall "as if the world was mine".'

SOPHIA LOREN (1934–)

❧ Invalid food ❧

When we are sick our appetites flag and we need to be tempted to eat lighter dishes that are easier on the digestive system. Served to us by Mum on a tray in our warm, snuggly beds, these 'invalid foods' are the ultimate comfort food:

❀ Alphabet soup – a thin soup containing small alphabet-shaped pasta.

❀ Thin slices of toast – lightly buttered.

❀ Soft-boiled egg with toast 'soldiers' (thin slices of toast to dip into the egg) – the epitome of comfort food, and so good for you!

❀ Jelly and ice cream – especially good for sore throats because it slides down so easily.

❀ Junket – a very old-fashioned pudding made with sweetened milk set with rennet; it's light and, like ice cream and jelly, it slides down the throat easily.

OLD MRS RABBIT

Who wouldn't like a mother like old Mrs Rabbit in Beatrix Potter's *The Tale of Peter Rabbit*? Mrs Rabbit has four children: Flopsy, Mopsy, Cottontail and Peter. Their mother tells her children not to get into any mischief while she is out. They can go into the fields or the lane but not into Mr McGregor's garden; their father had an accident there and ended up in one of Mr McGregor's pies. Flopsy, Mopsy and Cottontail, who are 'good little bunnies', go down the lane to pick blackberries. But Peter, the mischievous one, makes straight for the forbidden garden, where he stuffs himself with lettuce, French beans, radishes and parsley. Mr McGregor chases him and, in his frantic attempt to escape, Peter falls into a watering can and gets damp and cold.

That evening he's not very well. While his sisters have a supper of bread and milk and blackberries, Mrs Rabbit puts Peter to bed and makes some camomile tea with which she doses him: 'One teaspoonful to be taken at bed-time'.

Favourites with children the world over, Beatrix Potter's delightful creations are just the sort of stories mums read to their little invalids.

A mother's job

The job of being a mother involves so much more than just simple childcare. That's not even the half of it …

'A mother's place is in the wrong.'

CLAIRE RAYNER (1931–)

❊ To all applicants ❊

Nowadays, applicants for jobs usually find lists of 'duties and responsibilities' within the description of the position they are applying for. Just imagine what the job description for the position of 'Mother' might look like. Here are some of the duties it might entail.

A mother must:

❊   always wake in the middle of the night when her baby cries and get up to give a feed (prospective employees please note: this is not the responsibility of your partner who has acquired selective deafness and could therefore sleep through an earthquake)

❀ push a laden trolley around the supermarket, preferably with bored kids in tow

❀ cook the family meals

❀ be prepared for repeated demands for pizza and chips, accompanied by a refusal to eat anything else

❀ clean the house

❀ do the washing-up

❀ wash and iron clothes

❀ notice that the house needs cleaning (prospective employees please note: this is not the responsibility of your partner who has acquired selective blindness and simply does not see that dust on the stairs)

❀ minister to grazed knees

❀ wipe away tears

❀ read bedtime stories

❀ cuddle her children

❀ leave the office at a moment's notice when the school calls to say one of her kids has fallen

❋   take time off work to look after sick kids

❋   attend school meetings

❋   remind children to do their homework

❋   ask children why they have not done their homework

❋   remind children to pack their sports kit, homework,
      shoes, etc, for school the following day

❋   ask children why they forgot to pack their sports kit,
      homework, shoes

❋   be a taxi service for her children

❋   pick clothes up off the floor

❋   pick toys up off the floor

❋   trip over toys and shoes that have been left in the hall

❋   tell the kids – again – to tidy up

❋   tell the kids – again – that it is bedtime

❋   tell the kids – again – that 'That's enough television/
      computer games for now'

❋   tell the kids – again – to 'Turn that racket down'

❋   stay awake until her teenage children are safely back
      after a night out clubbing

❋ break up arguments between siblings

❋ develop a sniffer dog's instinct for digging out the truth in such statements as 'It wasn't me' and 'I didn't do it'

❋ plan and host children's birthday parties, forgetting how it felt as if Armageddon had swept through the house the last time she did it

❋ pretend that Santa exists

❋ answer all questions to the best of her ability, including such weighty philosophical issues as, 'Mum, is God real?', 'Why?' and 'Are we there yet?'

❋ remember all family birthdays and send cards and presents (prospective employees please note: this is not the responsibility of your partner who has acquired selective forgetfulness and will innocently answer 'Is it?' to the reminder that it will soon be his mother's birthday)

❋ give in to demands to get a kitten or puppy

❋ assume all the care of the kitten or puppy, now fully grown, when the kids leave home

❋ wonder whatever happened to 'me time'

❋ ignore how tired she is

❋ worry about her children

❋ feel guilty a lot of the time

❋ receive no income and have no holidays or sick leave

❋ do unlimited overtime

❋ do the job for love, not money

> 'The most remarkable thing about my mother is that for thirty years she served the family nothing but leftovers. The original meal has never been found.'
>
> CALVIN TRILLIN (1935–)

❦ Something to look forward to ❦

Research in the US shows that by the time a baby reaches the age of two, Mum (or Dad) will have changed his or her nappy 7,300 times. Fathers like to get it over with quickly, taking an average of 1 minute 36 seconds to whizz through the job, while mothers linger, needing 2 minutes 5 seconds – that's equivalent to three forty-hour working weeks in a year. No wonder mums get tired. Added to nappy changing, there are the broken nights, the terrible twos, toddlers with enough energy to power a rocket, the school run, hours of cooking, cleaning, feeding, acting as adjudicator in fights between siblings, and on and on. But never mind – there is light at the end of the tunnel, as *The Tired Woman's Epitaph* assures us:

Here lies a poor woman who was always tired;
She lived in a house where help was not hired.
Her last words on earth were: 'Dear Friends, I am going
Where washing ain't done, nor sweeping, nor sewing;
But everything there is exact to my wishes;
For where they don't eat there's no washing of dishes.
I'll be where loud anthems will always be ringing,
But, having no voice, I'll be clear of the singing.
Don't mourn for me now; don't mourn for me never —
I'm going to do nothing for ever and ever.'

'The joys of motherhood are never fully experienced
until the children are in bed.'

AUTHOR UNKNOWN

My mother says ...

Motherhood comes with its own vocabulary, a tried and tested range of responses that have been honed to pithy perfection down the generations. A mother is never lost for words – she has a vast armoury of verbal weapons ready to unleash, whatever the situation. 'I'll never say that to my children!' we vow but don't be too sure ... cringe we may, but as soon as we become mothers ourselves, the old familiar phrases just start popping out of our mouths, unbidden and uninvited.

❧ What our mothers say to us ❧

Witty, withering, illogical, contradictory, frustrating, annoying – here are some of the things our mothers say to us. Recognize any of them?

Mums on eating habits

❀ Don't talk with your mouth full.

❀ Be quiet and eat your supper.

❀ Eat your food – just think of all the starving children in the world.

❀ Eat your breakfast. You can't start the day on an empty stomach.

❀ If you're too full to finish your dinner, you're too full for treats.

❀ Eat your vegetables, they're good for you.

❀ But you just ate an hour ago!

❀ You look thin. Are you eating enough?

Mums on money

❀ Do you think I'm made of money?

❀ Money doesn't grow on trees.

❀ Turn off that light! Do you think I own the electricity company?

❀ Look after the pennies and the pounds will take care of themselves.

Mums on personal appearance

❊ If God had wanted you to have holes in your nose/tongue/eyebrows, he would have put them there.

❊ You're not dressed warmly enough.

❊ You're not going out dressed like *that*?

❊ Wash that muck off your face.

Mums on personal hygiene

❊ Put that down, you don't know where it's been.

❊ A little soap and water never killed anybody.

❊ Wash your hands.

❊ Wipe your feet.

❊ Brush your hair.

Mums on timekeeping

❊ Hurry up and get dressed – we haven't got all day!

❊ OK then, I'm going without you.

❊ Just wait till we get home.

❊ We're late!!!

Mums on personal responsibility

❋ Do you think your room will tidy itself?

❋ This isn't a hotel, you know.

❋ I'll treat you like an adult when you behave like one.

❋ You won't be happy till you break that, will you?

Mums on friends and siblings

❋ Your sister is allowed because she's older than you.

❋ I don't care who started it!

❋ Say sorry to your brother/sister.

❋ I don't care what your friend's mother says.

❋ I want you home by 10 o'clock.

❋ Will his/her parents be there?

❋ I don't care what 'everyone' is doing.

❋ I don't care if X's mother says she can.

❋ Who are these friends of yours anyway?

Mums on being gainfully occupied

❋   Don't you have anything better to do?

❋   How can you be bored? I was never bored at your age.

❋   You must have done *something* at school today – you can't have done 'nothing'!

❋   You can go out to play/watch television after you've done your homework/finished your meal/tidied your room...

❋   When I was a child ...

Mums on what to say

❋   Don't take that tone with me!

❋   Don't walk away when I'm talking to you.

❋   Now say you're sorry – and mean it.

❋   Wash your mouth out.

❋   I would never have talked to *my* mother like that!

❋   If you can't say something nice, don't say anything at all.

Mums on minding your manners

✻ Turn that racket down!

✻ I said *close* the door, not slam it.

Mums on who's in charge

✻ Why? Because I say so!

✻ How many times do I have to tell you?

✻ I'm going to count to three ... one, two ...

✻ Stop crying or I'll give you something to cry about.

✻ No means no.

✻ I'm not going to ask you again.

✻ What did I say the first time?

✻ Did you hear what I said?

✻ Ask your father.

✻ I'm doing this for your own good.

✻ You're grounded!

Mums on the enduring power of love

✻ You'll *always* be my baby.

❦ **Those magic words …** ❦

Children can give as good as they get and often display wit and wisdom beyond their years. Two of the most popular all-purpose ripostes are:

❋ I didn't ask to be born.

❋ It's not *faaair*!

When asked that favourite maternal question, 'What's the magic word?' (i.e. 'please'), one young boy I know quickly replied 'Abracadabra.' Well, of course it is.

My own two daughters have on occasion surprised me with their off-the-cuff remarks that cut right to the heart of the matter. Commenting on my compulsion for making lists of things I have to do, my younger daughter sagely observed: 'Don't make life a list.' And when they were old enough for me to stop being so directly involved as a mother and 'get a life' of my own, my older daughter fixed me with her calm gaze and told me, 'You can't hide behind your children any more.' Ouch.

When mum needs a boost

Everyone has an 'off day' now and again, days when the tasks ahead just seem insurmountable. But with the right attitude and the help of a few tricks that can make you feel good, you can consign those 'off days' to the dustbin. On the following pages you'll find some ideas that will pep you up and make you feel positive and ready to face any challenge.

Walk tall

Addressing your posture and body language is a great place to start boosting your confidence, as it's very easy and you'll feel the benefit almost instantly. Whatever your height and shape, your posture says a lot about you. Bad posture leads to all sorts of aches and strains, makes you appear smaller and less confident than you are. It can even prevent you from taking healthy deep breaths – so it's not surprising that correcting your posture will work wonders for your alertness and general wellbeing.

Try standing up with your shoulders back, your back straight and your chin tilted slightly upwards. This may feel forced at first, but persevere: the more you practise, the more natural it will feel – and the more relaxed *you* will feel. Keep this up everywhere you go, from the school run to the supermarket or office. You'll be surprised what a positive effect it has on you; before long, others will notice, too. If you also keep this in mind when you're sitting in front of your computer, you'll soon find yourself sitting in a much more upright position. This will lessen the strain on your back and shoulders as you type.

TIP

Imagine there's a string attached to the top of your head, and that an invisible puppeteer is gently pulling you upwards. It certainly works wonders for the supermodels ...

Be heard

Try speaking a little louder than you normally would. There's no need to shout, but be aware of speaking to be heard. Even if you feel as if your speech sounds exaggerated at first, work on speaking with a clear voice, and concentrate on this until you get to the point where speaking with clarity comes easily and naturally to you. You might even throw in a few casual hand gestures to emphasize your speech.

Another useful tactic is what some life coaches refer to as the 'fake-it-'til-you-make-it' approach, which essentially entails acting like someone with greater confidence. Though it might sound absurd, many people who have been advised to give it a go – for a nerve-wracking job interview, for instance – have reported a noticeable increase in actual confidence as a result of having faked it. After all, if fake confidence produces good results, you can only be encouraged by the experience, and by your own ability.

If you think this technique might be useful in your own life, approach it as if you were taking on the role of a confident version of yourself in a stage production. Taking on this new persona, and keeping it up for a few weeks, will in time lead you to assume the role automatically; in effect, you will have convinced yourself that you are a naturally confident person.

TIP

The key thing here is simply to augment your own confidence, not to transform yourself into someone who's totally unrecognizable to your husband, children, friends and colleagues. Introduce small changes one at a time, and you will gradually notice a positive difference.

❧ Give yourself a pat on the back ❧

Learn to appreciate your vast range of talents by focusing on the positive and not the negative. For the time being at least, forget the things you think you do badly and concentrate on the things you know you do well. Writing a self-appreciation list is a great way to get started. List all the positive adjectives that best describe you, and ask your friends and family to help when you run out of ideas. You might be surprised by the things that end up on your list: thoughtful, fun, creative, an attentive listener …

Next, write down all the things you are good at or that you manage to achieve in the course of a hectic day. Add to the list as often as you like and don't leave things out just because they seem commonplace or inconsequential; just as you praise your children for a job well done, pat yourself on the back as well.

❧ Confront your demons ❧

Whether or not you were a social butterfly when you were younger, keeping your social life going becomes considerably trickier when you have young children in tow. With so many balls in the air, something's got to give – and, more often than not, that 'something' is your nights out with your friends.

Lack of practice can leave you feeling as if you've forgotten how to be the life and soul of the party, but practice makes perfect. If you're nervous about a night out with a group of people you don't know very well, brush up on your current affairs when the kids are at school or in bed or read an up-to-date magazine on your way there.

Don't give in to anxiety and let lack of practice age you prematurely. When trying new things, remember that the vast majority of people want you to succeed – put your best foot forward and get on with it.

❈ Don't worry, be happy ❈

Don't underestimate the power of happiness: make time to be happy. This may sound ludicrous, but stop and think about it. Would you say you are a happy person? Or are you just too busy even to notice? Well, you should think about it because your own happiness can have a profound effect on your family's happiness. A study by the University of Edinburgh found that 50 per cent of a person's happiness is partly an inherited characteristic and partly formed during childhood, while the other 50 per cent is down to the individual and his or her environment. In a nutshell: if you're feeling unhappy, you can do something about it. Everyone deserves to feel happy and everyone needs to have some chill-out time. If you set some time aside for this, you'll soon see that it improves the quality of your home life.

TOP 5 HAPPY TIPS

❀ Set aside as much time as you can to immerse yourself in something you really enjoy. Whether it's an outdoor hobby or getting your hair done, you should spend time indulging in something that helps you unwind.

❀ Surround yourself with good company whenever you can. If you don't have the time or energy to host dinner parties, invite friends or family over for a casual evening – each person can bring an easy dish while you provide popcorn, wine and a DVD.

❀ Be open and honest with people you are close to for more rewarding relationships.

❀ Spend quality time with your family outside your home. Go to the park, spend a day on the beach, visit a castle ... Whatever it is you all enjoy, just go out and have fun.

❀ Control negative thoughts by turning them on their head and doing something positive to rectify them.

Just Say No

It's very easy to feel duty-bound to sort out everybody else's happiness before your own, but before long you can find yourself running endless errands and performing endless favours, none of which you'd choose to do if you had the option. How can you possibly make the most of your free time when there's a lunch to attend, or a work party at which you ought to show your face? There is one simple, incredibly empowering answer to all these questions: just say no.

We've all been in the situation where we've grudgingly said, 'Yes, I'll be there' or, 'OK, I suppose I'm going in that direction anyway', when what we really want to say is, 'To be honest, I can't think of anything I want to do less.' While our intentions are admirable when we agree to do things just to make other people happy, the downside is rising resentment and stress.

Feeling empowered is all about setting boundaries and sticking to them. I'm not suggesting we always put ourselves first no matter what – nor that we actually go around saying, 'To be honest, I can't think of anything I want to do less' – but simply that we become selective with the precious free time we have. It is perfectly acceptable to say 'no' if it's done tactfully.

TIP

It's probably best to introduce any changes in your general attitude gradually, lest your friends or colleagues become offended at your sudden lack of enthusiasm, but try it once and see how it feels.

Listen and learn

It's easy to forget that the art of conversation isn't all about talking: there's not much point in someone talking if nobody's actually listening. We all have days where we feel disinclined or uninspired to make sparkling, witty conversation, so why not simply listen to those who are in the mood for holding court? After all, everyone loves talking about themselves. If you can prove yourself a good listener by asking questions and interjecting with the occasional 'How awful!' or 'What was he thinking?', the other person will come away from the conversation thinking they've had a great chat. And, what's more, they'll probably prove just as attentive next time you feel like launching into an anecdote.

Have fun

When was the last time you did something for the simple reason that it interested you? Too many of us let our interests or hobbies slide because we think we don't have time or because we get used to being too busy. But we're never too busy to collect the kids from school, take them to clubs, and shop for presents for their friends' parties, are we? We make the time to do those things because they are important, but why is it different when it comes to our own needs? Are you a craving culture vulture? You may not have quite as much time to spare these days, but it's vital to keep a strong sense of your own individual personality despite your other obligations. Being glamorous isn't just about looking the part: you need to feel like a rounded, interesting person, too.

✤ Be a copycat ✤

Try emulating someone you admire. This doesn't mean be an outright copycat, but if there's someone whose poise or style you envy, study her (in a non-stalking manner) to work out what she does differently. Does she speak in an engaging manner or carry herself elegantly? Does her body language radiate confidence? Is her tone understanding or her outfit carefully chosen? These are all things you can try yourself. Take some time to observe these traits and see if you can incorporate a unique take on any of them into your own personal style.

You can't phone, you can't visit?

Outspoken, interfering, opinionated, overbearing, tactless – and at the same time warm, loving and fiercely devoted to her family – the Jewish mother is a gift to drama and comedy.

❊ The Jewish mother ❊

She can be wonderful or she can be maddening – here are some of the most memorable examples of her as seen by advertisers and filmmakers.

Oy vey!

Back in the late 1980s and early 1990s, British telecommunications giant BT (British Telecom) produced one of the most successful television advertising campaigns. Each ad was a mini-story in itself and featured British actress and comedian Maureen Lipman in her priceless characterization as a stereotypical Jewish mother and grandmother by the name of Beattie (B-T – get it?).

In one ad, we see Beattie sitting in an armchair, embroidering while she talks to a framed photograph of her son. 'So you can't phone? You can't pick up the phone and dial? You got maybe something wrong with your finger?' she demands of the picture. Cut to a shot of fingers tapping out her number – it's her son Melvin. 'Hello mum,' he says. Cut to Beattie after the call. She smiles and looks at the picture again: 'So you can't visit? You can only phone? Never mind, it's a pleasure to hear your voice… [pause] …a little more often wouldn't hurt.'

In another ad, Melvin calls to say he's been held up at work and will be an hour late for dinner. 'Your sister's never late,' Beattie says, and then, 'I'll come down, I'll bring you a sandwich – I'll bring you a jumper!' Melvin doesn't want either; he works in a modern airconditioned building, he says. 'You didn't *tell* me it was airconditioned! Some children *talk* to their parents. Now, what do you want in your sandwich?'

> 'My mother phones daily to ask, "Did you just try to reach me?" When I reply "No," she adds, "So, if you're not too busy, call me while I'm still alive," and hangs up.
>
> ERMA BOMBECK (1927–96)

Enough already

'Oedipus complex' was a term used by Sigmund Freud to describe a stage in psychosexual development when a young child, according to Freud, feels sexual desire for the parent of the opposite sex and rivalry with the parent of the same sex. The name comes from an ancient Greek tragedy, written by Sophocles, in which Oedipus Rex (or Oedipus the King) discovers that he has unknowingly killed his own father and married his mother.

Woody Allen's short comedy *Oedipus Wrecks* is a witty play on words and on the idea of the mother-dominated son … in this case, the Jewish-mother- dominated son. Allen plays Sheldon Mills, a lawyer who has been browbeaten and embarrassed by his mother all his life. In an early scene with his therapist (you can't have a Woody Allen film without an analyst somewhere), Sheldon admits that he would like his mother to 'simply disappear'. He describes how he has dreamt that she died and how, while he was driving the hearse to the cemetery, she is shouting directions at him from inside her coffin: 'Take a left, you're going the long route. And slow up, d'ya have to speed? If ya gonna be nasty, I'm not goin'!'

Mother isn't pleased to meet Sheldon's fiancée Lisa (Mia Farrow); not only is she a divorcée with three children but worse – she's a goy, a *shiksa*, a non-Jew. But she still takes the time to show Lisa naked baby pictures of Sheldon and describe how he used to wet his bed.

Sheldon doesn't know it but his wish to have his mother disappear is shortly to be fulfilled. He and Lisa and her children take her to a magic show, where she is chosen by the magician to participate in a disappearing trick. The trick works so well that she really does vanish – only to reappear, as a huge, disembodied face floating over the New York skyline and sharing the secrets of her son's private life with the population of the city.

Mazel tov

A much warmer and more cuddly version of the Jewish mother was played by Barbra Streisand in the 2004 comedy film *Meet the Fockers*. Barbra plays Roz, a sex therapist who counsels senior citizens – a kind of middle-aged, hippy-style version of 'Dr Ruth' (Ruth Westheimer), the diminutive media celebrity sex therapist. Roz writes books with titles like *Meet Your Orgasm*!, collects erotic ethnic carvings and is wife to stay-at-home dad Bernie (Dustin Hoffman) and mother to Greg (Ben Stiller) who has brought his fiancée Pam and her parents to meet his parents for the first time. The differences between the two families – the liberal, uninhibited, touchy-feely Fockers and the conservative and reserved Byrnes (especially ex-CIA control freak Jack Byrnes, played by Robert de Niro) – provide plenty of material for comedy. But perhaps Greg's most embarrassing moment is when his mother insists on getting out the photo album – yes, more baby pictures. 'That's Greg getting circumcised,' she explains to Dina, Pam's mother. 'Don't tell me you've kept his umbilical cord too?' says Dina, seeing a little scrap of skin tucked into the album. 'No, that's Greg's ...' The word 'foreskin' hangs in the air.

'A Freudian slip is where you say one thing but mean your mother.'

AUTHOR UNKNOWN

Well presented

Children are naturally creative and will really enjoy making presents for other people – and how proud they will feel at Granny's delight with the gift they have made specially for her. For mums, too, making homemade presents opens a door to those forgotten, old-fashioned crafts that can bring great pleasure for such little cost. Here are a few ideas for you to suggest to your child … you may have to lend a hand, too!

❋ A picture in a frame ❋

A family photo in a frame is such an easy present to make, yet it can mean so much to the recipient. One of the most treasured gifts I have ever given was one to my nephew. I found an old photograph of his mother when she was in her twenties. I had a good-quality copy made of the original and then had it professionally framed, and gave it to him for his fortieth birthday. He was so moved – his mother had died when he was only fourteen, so her picture had special meaning for him and took pride of place among his presents.

You don't need to go to the expense of professional framing. Simple frames, to take A4- or A5-sized images, are easily available and very reasonably priced. If it's an old photograph and you don't want to sacrifice the original, you can have it copied or even scanned – the technology is so good now that you'll hardly be able to tell the difference. The other advantage of a copy or a scan is that you can have the image enlarged and reduced to suit the size of the frame.

Here comes the fun bit

The fun bit for kids lies in the decorating of the frame, so it's best to buy an untreated pine one (they cost less too). The options for decoration are huge – the frame can be painted a plain colour, or stencilled, or adorned with patterns, drawings and glitter. The decoration will need to be reasonably hardwearing, so avoid paper stickers that may peel off in time. The decorating should be done *before* the picture is inserted in the frame so that it is not damaged by paint or glitter. And, if the kids are old enough, they may be receptive to a little good taste and may agree to ditch that combination of glaring red and orange in favour of something more subtle that won't completely overwhelm the picture.

❊ Another picture in a frame ❊

Photographs aren't the only things that can go in a frame – kids' drawings and paintings can too. Artwork done at school or at home moves up into a different category when set off by a frame. I still have a couple of drawings my younger daughter did for me and framed as gifts. As a fairly broke student, she couldn't afford much but the thought that went into these personal presents made them worth so much more than their material cost.

Another idea kids might like is to draw the letters of the recipient's name on a piece of paper, then fill them in with paint, using pattern and decorative motifs such as leaves, flowers and butterflies – or whatever takes their fancy. Mounted in a suitable frame, these can make a lovely, personalized gift.

❊ Photo album ❊

A book of photographic memories is something that older members of the family will treasure. Purpose-made photo albums look smart but are altogether too 'grown-up' for kids. Far better to buy a scrapbook or one of those notebooks with thick, coloured (possibly handmade) pages inside. If kids are using a scrapbook, they might need to cover the outside with paper to make it look more attractive.

Before sticking the photographs into the book, kids could think how they want to arrange them – in chronological order, perhaps, or by category (grouping all the pictures of a sibling together, for example) or location (all of us on that holiday in Spain).

When the photos are in place, make sure they are captioned with the name of the people in the pictures plus, if possible, location and date (month or year) – the latter is important as the recipients will want to locate the memories in time.

❧ Jewel casket ❧

The keepsake box on page 136 will make a lovely present, as will a trinket or jewellery casket. A large matchbox is ideal for this – it is reasonably robust and the outer sleeve slides back and forth easily, so there are no fiddly bits that might break off. Large matchboxes often have a card divider in the middle to separate the interior into two compartments; you can leave this in or remove it, as you wish.

The first step is to paint the inside and outside of the box, which will make it even stronger. The real creativity is reserved for adorning the sliding sleeve – kids can really go to town here and aim for the most sumptuous, Aladdin's Cave effect. First, they should cover the outside of the sleeve with wrapping paper (gold or silver in the pattern would be good), gluing it into place neatly. The top can now be decorated with beads, sequins, decorative buttons, small Christmas tree baubles – anything that will make it look opulent – attached with glue and tape. For extra luxury, the base of the inside of the box can be lined with tissue paper.

❦ Wrapping it up ❦

Now that the kids have made their presents, it's time to wrap them up – whatever our age, nothing beats the excitement of wondering what's inside the wrapped bundle we've been given. Always try to remember to save wrappings, trimmings, bows, ribbons etc from birthday and Christmas gifts and recycle them imaginatively – being creative with wrappings can be great fun for both children and adults.

Wrapping paper

Sophisticated urbanites might go for minimal brown wrapping paper, tied with tasteful raffia – but that's much too restrained for most children. Instead, they can turn ordinary brown paper into a riot of pattern by applying colourful potato prints. Or they could cut out motifs from used wrapping paper and stick them to the brown paper (it's better to attach the motifs after the present has been wrapped, or they may end up in a fold and peel off).

❧ Mini-boxes ❧

Unless they have come in their own bespoke boxes, it's always difficult to know how to package small gift items like rings or earrings securely. Small matchboxes, painted and decorated, are an inspired solution. If there's enough space, the base of the matchbox can be lined with tissue paper or cotton wool to allow the contents to nestle snugly inside.

Ribbon coils

Trimmings are the one element that make all the difference between an ordinary package and a great gift parcel. Ribbon coils add a look of professionalism to any wrapping, and they are fun to do — and easy, once you get the hang of it. Simply stretch out the loose ends of a bow, or a separate length of ribbon and run the closed blades of the scissors quickly down it. The ribbon will spring back like a corkscrew.

'No matter how old you get, if you can keep the desire to be creative, you're keeping the man-child alive.'

JOHN CASSAVETES (1929–89)

Gift tags

Save your greetings cards and cut them down to make gift tags for the presents you give. The festive scenes from the fronts of Christmas cards work really well as next year's gift tags. Simply cut out the Santa or Christmas tree, punch a hole in an appropriate place and add string or ribbon to attach — *et voilà!*

The good, the bad
and the ditzy

Like a bag of mixed sweets, mothers come in many different varieties. They may be positively saintly or as mean as Cruella de Ville – in books and films anyway. Our real flesh-and-blood mothers are likely to be a mixture of many different traits.

❋ The good ... ❋

She's patient, kind but firm, never complains, is quietly resilient in the face of adversity (which she usually has in bucketfuls) and, despite the hardships of her life, she always has time to play with her children, read to them and give them buns for tea. So who is this paragon of perfection, this saint? She is the ideal – or rather idealized – mother. Unfortunately, you're more likely to meet her on the pages of fictional stories than in real life. Here are some examples:

Little Women

'Marmee', or Margaret March, was the mother of Meg, Jo, Beth and Amy in Louisa May Alcott's *Little Women*, published in 1868–69. While her husband is away serving as a chaplain for the Union Army in the American Civil War, Marmee acts as head of the household. The family has fallen on hard times because, it is implied, 'Father' March (a man of high morals, naturally) has helped out some friends who were in debt. But despite their poverty, Marmee remains a tower of strength, exemplifying all those 'old-fashioned virtues' of hard work, integrity and charity.

The Railway Children

Like Marmee, Mother in Edith Nesbit's *The Railway Children*, published in 1906, is made of strong stuff – but in the most ladylike way. After her husband is imprisoned (falsely, of course) for selling state secrets to the Russians, she and her children – Roberta, Peter and Phyllis – have to leave the security of their suburban home for a rundown house near a railway line in the country. The sole breadwinner, Mother gets down to writing and selling stories to earn money. But she still finds time to play with the children, read to them, help them with homework and write poems to celebrate special occasions like the christening of some new kittens or the refurnishing of the doll's house. Treats and presents are in short supply but when she sells a story about 'the King of the Mussels', she is able to buy the children buns for tea.

The Waltons

Who could forget the Waltons, the popular American TV series featuring John and Olivia Walton and their seven children? Struggling to survive during the Great Depression and World War II, Olivia at least has a husband to help her manage, unlike poor single parents Marmee and Mother. With a brood of seven to manage, she does an exemplary job, being loving and kind but consistent and firm, too – just the way a 'good mother' should. Like Marmee and Mother, Olivia has a strong charitable streak too. A devout Baptist, she often takes in friends or strangers in need.

❊ The bad ... ❊

Wicked stepmothers! They abound in folk and fairy tales, and nowhere is there a more grisly collection than in the stories of the Brothers Grimm. In the tale entitled *The Juniper Tree*, a widower's second wife cannot bear her stepson, whose mother lies buried under the eponymous tree. She resolves to get rid of him so that her own daughter does not have to share any inheritance that may be coming her way. After tricking the little lad into looking into an apple storage chest, she slams the lid down on him, lopping off his head; she then serves him up as a succulent stew. Of course, with a bit of magic all comes right in the end. The remains of the boy turn into a songbird – that trills the inimitable lines: 'My mother she killed me, my father he ate me...' – which then has the satisfaction of dropping a millwheel onto his wicked stepmother, crushing her to death.

In *Hansel and Gretel*, the Brothers don't sugar the pill – it is the children's own mother, not their stepmother, who is the driving force in persuading their father to abandon them in the forest because there isn't enough food to feed the whole family.

It's a hard life ...

Dead mothers, heartless new wives, absentee fathers (just where was Cinderella's dad during all her trials?). Not a pretty picture, but in fact some of the themes of these stories reflect social history. Before modern obstetrics, many women did die in childbirth or from complications not long after, so men often took second wives. For the women, marriage offered a way out of hardship and potential destitution.

In the world of these 'tales of the hearth' though, men don't get much of a look-in. The drama is set firmly in the domestic sphere, the realm of women, which perhaps helps to answer the puzzling question: why did the fathers never have a clue as to what is going on within the family and why did they never intervene?

❦ … and the ditzy ❦

In some cases it's hard to know who's the grown-up and who's the child … No ditzy mother worth her salt can claim to have done a good job unless she has at some time made her children cringe.

Bridget Jones

The eponymous heroine of the books and films has a delightfully dotty mother who – according to her daughter – thinks that a gherkin is the height of sophistication. When Bridget offers to call her on her mobile phone, her mother replies, 'Mobile, darling? Don't be silly – you haven't had one of those since you were about four. Don't you remember? With little fishes on?' On another occasion, she phones Bridget in the middle of summer to ask her what she wants for Christmas. Actually, it's a ploy to get Bridget to attend the annual New Year's Day turkey curry buffet, regularly hosted by friends of hers, so that her daughter can meet the eligible Mark Darcy. 'Mark, you remember Bridget?' she says by way of introduction. 'She used to run around your lawn with no clothes on, remember?'

Absolutely Fabulous

In the British TV hit comedy series *Absolutely Fabulous*, fast-living Edina boozes, behaves outrageously and is obsessed with fashion, while her sensible, spectacle-wearing daughter Saffy dresses conservatively and has a strong moral sense.

She is constantly disapproving of her mother's behaviour and, more especially, that of her mother's friend Patsy.

❋ The yummy mummy ❋

In the prosperous nineties, a new species appeared on the scene. She was skinny, glossy and ultra-fashionable. She wore huge designer sunglasses, drove an SUV, didn't work, drank skinny lattes in smart cafés with others of her kind, and often sported the perfect accessory — a smartly turned-out infant or toddler. Who was she? The yummy mummy, of course.

Love her, hate her ...

How we love to hate the yummy mummy. Her clothes are never stained with baby food like those of mere mortal mums, her figure is as slim and toned as before pregnancy, she never seems to have shadows under her eyes through exhaustion, is never seen without full make-up, and seems to possess an ample supply of that thing that other mothers have in such short supply — time. How on earth does she manage it? Well, money has a lot to do with it. Real yummy mummies are able to afford an army of nannies and other kinds of domestic help so that they can be stay-at-home mums without getting their hands dirty or breaking a single perfectly manicured nail.

Famous yummies

It takes time and money to be a real yummy mummy, which is why so many ultra-yummies are celebs. Perhaps the most famous one is Victoria Beckham – but there are many more:

* Angelina Jolie

* Gwyneth Paltrow

* Gwen Stefani

* Heidi Klum

* Jerry Hall

* Kate Beckinsale

* Katie Holmes

* Liz Hurley

* Lulu

* Halle Berry

* Nicole Kidman

* Sharon Stone

* Susan Sarandon

* Twiggy

How to be a yummy mummy

OK, so we don't all have movie star incomes, banker husbands so we can be stay-at-home mothers, or model girl looks (or the money to spend on cosmetic surgery, even if we wanted to), but we can take a tip or two from the yummy mummy. To give her her due, she does have standards. Just because she has kids, it doesn't mean that she doesn't want to go on looking after herself and looking good – and who wouldn't want to do that?

Grooming is very important to the yummy mummy, but she is far from the first to priortize this. For those of us old enough to remember, mums pre- and post-World War II would never dream of going out without their hair done and some lippy on.

Nor need age be a barrier. While she is generally thought of as being under thirty-five, a mother can be a yummy mummy – or indeed a glamorous granny – however old she is (see 'Glam-mas' on page 113). And you don't need oodles of cash either. What mums probably lack most is time, just to relax and pamper themselves. Here are some easy and relatively inexpensive ways to achieve that 'me time' and to bring out the yummy mummy in every mother:

❋ **Haircut**

Of all the beauty treatments a mum can have, a professional shampoo and cut reap the greatest rewards. Just having an hour to herself is heaven; relaxing back while the hairdresser gently shampoos and massages her head releases all that tension; and a good haircut, styled to suit her face, age and personality, can transform her appearance in an instant and take years off her. If budget allows for only one beauty treatment, let this be it.

❊ Manicure

All those celeb yummy mummies have immaculate nails, so a professional manicure is a lovely pampering treat once in a while. But if this is beyond your budget or schedule, a home manicure can be almost as nice. Get all the ingredients together – base coat, varnish, top coat, cuticle oil, varnish remover, emery boards, orange sticks, cotton wool – set aside time with no interruptions, and enjoy! For everyday wear, long red nails are out; they will chip in no time and look horrible. To be an understated yummy mummy, clean, well-shaped, well-cared-for nails and clear varnish are the best option.

❊ Perfume

A splash of scent is an instant pick-me-up. Luxurious, feminine and indulgent, it's a must-have for every yummy mummy.

❊ Lipstick

Lippy is up there with a good haircut as an essential beautifier. Busy mums may not have time for the full slap, but a quick slick of lipstick is a shortcut to glamour. It takes a second to apply and brings colour and prettiness to the face. There are so many varieties to choose from nowadays, from clear and tinted glosses to rich, colourful creams and sticks, that you are bound to find one to suit personal taste and lifestyle – a great present for any mum.

❋ **Pretty underwear**

It's easy enough to do. We buy underwear and then – because it is *under* wear and is hidden by our clothes – we forget about it and keep it long past its sell-by date, when it has turned from white to grey and lost its elasticity. Now's the time to ditch it! No self-respecting yummy mummy would wear anything less than the prettiest, sexiest undies. Just because it isn't on public view doesn't mean that you should put up with drab bras and knickers. So go on, get out there and check out the gorgeous array of items on offer. (A word of advice here: if you haven't checked your bra size in a while, it's wise to be professionally measured. Many women wear bras that are either too big or too small for them, and bust sizes change, too, with age and at different times of the month. Most good department stores offer a free bra-fitting service.)

❋ Bling

A little bit of bling can do any mum a world of good. We are not talking diamonds here. Whether ethnic-style or glamorous glitter, there is a wealth of reasonably priced jewellery available out there. A pair of earrings, a bracelet or necklace popped on when getting dressed in the morning, can make a statement: 'I care about how I look. I am making an effort. I matter.' Go on, mum, treat yourself every now and again and, coming up to your birthday, make sure to drop the odd hint to family and friends.

❋ Facial

This is the ultimate luxury – being pampered in a beauty salon. There are various options on offer, from the traditional facial to treatments using electrical impulses that claim to give a mini-facelift by tightening the facial muscles. Combined with the soothing atmosphere of the salon and a beautician ministering to you as if you were Cleopatra herself, a facial is a sure route to heaven.

If money is tight, there are plenty of products on sale that allow you to have a home beauty treatment at a fraction of the cost charged by the salons. The trick here is to emulate the salon experience – and that means no multi-tasking, like doing the washing up while that hot mud mask does its work. This is supposed to be a luxury. Allow a good hour, with no distractions and interruptions. Light some candles, burn some incense or perfumed oil, and put on some gentle music. These will all create the right mood to ensure that the experience is as relaxing and pleasurable as possible.

❊ **Lunch**

Yummy mummies love to do lunch. Why not copy them and set a special date for a mum's lunch? The food will cost money, but every now and again it's a wonderful treat to spend time with friends we love, and hang the expense! You might enjoy it so much that you make it a regular occasion.

❊ Glam-mas ❊

At some point in their lives, the children of yummy mummies become parents themselves and the YMs move into another category – not *grand*mas but *glam*-mas. Here are a few glamorous grannies, to inspire … and there's not a zimmer frame in sight:

❊ Blythe Danner (mother of Gwyneth Paltrow)

❊ Catherine Deneuve

❊ Dayle Haddon (American model)

❊ Goldie Hawn

❋ Jackie Adams (mother of Victoria Beckham)

❋ Jane Fonda

❋ Jo Wood (former wife of Rolling Stone Ronnie Wood)

❋ Sophia Loren

❋ Tina Turner

Stress-busting tips for busy mums

The best way for a busy mum to tackle stress is by doing a thorough stock-take of her life and arranging things in a more efficient way. Here are some ideas about how to do that – highlighting different ways of organizing yourself so as to avoid a bottleneck of unmanageable tasks.

❧ Make lists ❧

There's nothing like a 'to-do' list to keep track of all the things you need to achieve on a daily basis. But scrappy lists on the backs of envelopes and left all over the house can be trouble. The trick is to have a designated place for your 'to-do' list – whether it's in a diary, Filofax or mobile phone – rather than scribbling things down here and there. Take five minutes at the end of each day to cross off the things you've done and add any new tasks for the next day.

Other rolling lists that prove invaluable are Christmas and birthday-present lists – if you see something during the course of the year and know your child would love it for

Christmas, write it down before you forget. Likewise, keep a note of any ideas for fun days out or birthday-party themes that come to you in a flash of inspiration.

✺ Prioritize ✺

Prioritize the things on your 'to-do' list according to what is most urgent or time-sensitive. If you have a particularly busy week – let's say you're getting ready for a family holiday – the time you might have spent cleaning the house

---

TOP 3 KITCHEN TIPS

✳ If you don't own a vegetable steamer but fancy steaming your greens for a change, use a metal colander instead. Put the prepared vegetables into the colander, place it on top of a pan of boiling water, and cover the whole lot with a lid. But be careful: it will become very hot.

✳ To prevent a smelly bin, put a solid air-freshener in the bottom of the bin (before putting the bag in). It'll keep your kitchen free of rubbishy odours for weeks.

✳ Restore shine to a stainless-steel sink and taps by rubbing a touch of vinegar over the surface. Leave for about an hour and then buff with kitchen towel for a shiny finish.

---

from top to bottom might be better spent ironing and packing cases. The cleaning is a low priority in this situation, and unfortunately will still be there when you get back. If there's one particular job that's causing you to worry, address that first and fit the lesser things around it.

Don't be a slave to routine

Some mums live by routine from the moment they get up to the moment they go to bed. While establishing a routine can help create order in a hectic household and is useful for certain things – such as leaving the house on time every morning – it's important to accept that routines, like rules, will be broken every now and then, to avoid becoming anxious when this inevitably happens. If routine were adhered to slavishly, there would never be any time for spontaneous fun or the sort of last-minute changes of plan that become necessary when your child develops toothache and has to stay at home.

Routine can seem the only way to manage when both parents work, but a bit of common sense can make the schedule flow in a less regimented way. Instead of insisting the kids are in bed by 8pm on the dot, relax things a bit by widening the bedtime window to, say, between 7.45 and 8.30. That way, any unforeseen circumstances shouldn't derail the whole evening and leave you feeling as if you've let things slip. Excitable children and strict schedules simply don't mix well – don't be hard on yourself.

❧ Work when you're most productive ❧

If you tend to be more alert and energetic in the mornings, aim to get the bulk of your work done then, with lighter tasks saved for the afternoon slump, and any tasks that can be fitted around feeding, playing with and washing children saved for the evening. If you're half asleep in the mornings but full of beans after lunch, plan your jobs around that.

Most people's natural body clocks make them feel energized in the mornings until around midday, and then again in the early evening. This is probably the ideal energy-distribution to have, as it gives you the later evening off to relax.

❧ Detoxify your surroundings ❧

Whether or not you follow the principles of feng shui when it comes to arranging your furniture and plants, there's a lot to be said for everything having its place. If you're surrounded by clutter as you try to go about your daily jobs, you're bound to become needlessly stressed. Whether it's a permanent pile of papers on the dining room table or a gaggle of ornaments that only gather dust, target the clutter and make dealing with it a priority.

Are you a hoarder? If you can't bear to part with the various objects that are cluttering up your life, invest in some decent storage boxes that can be filled systematically and stored in the garage or under the stairs. Take an extra ten minutes to label each box as accurately as possible — if you can't face sorting out the clutter, at least know where every item or document is.

If, on the other hand, the situation's become so dire that you need a thorough spring clean, try to give everything a designated home and make sure everyone knows about it. Keep paperwork and stationery away from areas they have no business invading — the top of the microwave, for instance — and make it your children's job to put DVDs and computer games back in their cases when they've finished with them, rather than allowing things to pile up into a towering mess.

✲ Embrace Plan B ✲

Even with your to-do list firmly in hand, not everything will go to plan. Say a friend calls you on a Friday morning and suggests meeting for lunch that same day, but you have a pile of ironing and all the cleaning in front of you — what do you do? The answer is quite simple: forget the ironing for now and fit in the areas most in need of a once-over before and after your lunch, or when you have a few minutes here and there over the weekend. Unless you're expecting a visiting dignitary (the mother-in-law, for instance), the house doesn't have to be entirely spotless every weekend.

If you can't achieve Plan A for whatever reason, embrace Plan B instead. Lord knows there's more to life than rules and routines, so go out and enjoy your lunch date or make the most of some unexpected good weather.

Have a healthy mind in a healthy body

The Roman poet Juvenal decreed that 'mens sana in corpore sano' ('a healthy mind in a healthy body') was one of the most desirable things in life, and his advice couldn't be more relevant to busy mums today. If you look after yourself properly, you'll have a more positive outlook on things, which in turn will massively reduce your susceptibility to stress.

So if there's anything in your diet or exercise regimes (or lack of…) that causes you to feel uneasy, uncomfortable or unattractive, try cutting it out. Does that second coffee give you the jitters? Did that late-night piece of cake leave you sleepless and too full of energy? Does your expensive gym membership make you feel guilty every time you skip a session? Cut them out –or substitute them for less stress-inducing things – and see if you feel more energetic and positive.

TIP

Unused gym memberships are one of the most stress-inducing commodities of modern times. If ever it gets to the stage where you've skipped a whole month for no apparent reason but yet you can't see yourself going back any time soon, hold your head up high and quit. Think of all the fabulous fun you could have with the money you save …

Maintain a healthy life-work-play balance

When you have had a chance to incorporate some of these tips into your routine, take time to make sure you have the balance right. Do you have enough time for your children, your husband, your friends and – most importantly – yourself, or are you still run ragged? If you feel the balance isn't quite right, make some adjustments based on your personal circumstances. Your household priorities will be affected by whether you have a day job or regular evening commitments, whether you socialize a lot during the day or have some help around the house, and whether your children are out at school or need near-constant attention.

Don't increase your stress levels, tailor your agenda to your lifestyle and keep tweaking it until it runs like clockwork – albeit with the occasional unexpected cuckoo.

Brave mums

Mothers aren't all about home and apple pie. Some have shown true courage and determination in their lives, especially in caring for their children – and often for the children of others. A few of their remarkable stories are recorded here.

✳ Mothers of the Disappeared ✳

Perhaps some of the most famous mothers in the world are the Mothers of the Plaza de Mayo, in Argentina. During what was known as Argentina's Dirty War (1976–83), thousands of people were abducted by government agents, never to be seen again. In response, the mothers of the missing held their first demonstration on the Plaza de Mayo in central Buenos Aires, in front of the Casa Rosada presidential palace, on 30 April 1977. Ever since then, the women – now known as the Mothers of the Plaza de Mayo and wearing white headscarves with their children's names written on them – have continued to gather in the square every week, to protest against the disappearance of their sons and daughters and to demand that they be reunited with them, or at least to know their fate. Their dignity, courage and strength sum up the best attributes of motherhood.

❧ Maternal instinct ❧

After a devastating earthquake in China in 2008, Jiang Xiaojuan, a police officer and twenty-nine-year-old mother of a baby son, reported for duty. During the destruction, many babies had either been separated from their mothers or orphaned. From the rubble, all Jiang could hear were hungry infants crying. This was when her maternal instincts kicked in. She breast-fed the babies, at one point feeding as many as nine. Jiang thought nothing of what she had done: 'It is a mother's reaction and a basic duty as a police officer to help,' she said. The media thought otherwise, however, and named her 'China's Mother No. 1'.

❧ That's the way to do it! ❧

The Vietnamese authorities know how to honour the mothers of their nation. Due to be finished in 2011, a giant stone statue dedicated to thousands of heroic Vietnamese mothers is under construction, funded (at huge expense) by donations from the people of the country. Standing 18.5m

(61ft) tall and more than 24m (78ft) deep, it contains a memorial and a stone stele featuring the names of nearly 50,000 mothers. In the square in front of the statue, eight pillars, each 9m (29ft) high, are carved with the stories of heroic mothers from different parts of Vietnam. The statue itself is modelled on Nguyen Thi Thu, a woman whose nine children, one son-in-law and one grandchild were killed in Vietnam's revolutionary wars.

❊ The ultimate sacrifice ❊

There are countless stories of Jewish mothers whose bravery and sacrifice helped to save their children during the Nazi period in Germany and Eastern Europe. Some sent their children away for safety to countries such as Great Britain, knowing that they might never see them again. They themselves perished in the concentration camps but their sacrifice meant that their children survived. Other children of the Holocaust tell how their mothers saved their own food for them – such as scraps of bread that they kept back and eked out to their children during the day so that the young ones would not go hungry. In the most horrendous of circumstances, mother love remains strong and true, whatever the cost.

❧ My children's children ❧

You'd think that by the time you became a granny your mothering days would be over. In Africa, this was once the stage of life where – having cared for and brought up your children – you could expect them to return the favour and look after you. Not so now. For many elderly African women, AIDS has turned tradition on its head. As their sons and daughters die of the disease, thousands of grannies find themselves doing what they thought they would never have to do: become surrogate mothers to their orphaned grandchildren.

The numbers of AIDS orphans are staggering. In 2006 in Swaziland, official statistics give a figure of around 60,000, while in 2009, aid workers in Zimbabwe reported that some grannies were looking after as many as fifteen children. Surviving family members try to help, but it is often left to the grannies – affectionately known in Swaziland as Gogos – to pick up pieces. Ageing, poor and uneducated, these remarkable women are the glue that keeps it all together.

Having it all

It is truly extraordinary the distance women (in the West at any rate) have travelled. A century or so ago, men claimed all the legal rights – over property, over their wives, over their children. Wives were financially dependent on their husbands and couldn't even vote. It was considered 'unfeminine' for a woman to be educated and informed; worse still, such unladylike traits would put off potential husbands – and then what fate awaited you? Being an unmarried, childless governess. Now, women have families and their own careers too.

✢ A woman's place … ✢

… is in the home. But not for these ladies, who managed to combine motherhood with great success in their respective fields. Here's a random list of just a few Alpha Mothers:

❋ Anita Roddick, founder of ethical beauty chain Body Shop

❋ Barbara Hepworth, internationally renowned abstract sculptor

❋ Catherine the Great, feisty Russian Empress

❋ Dorothea Christiane Erxleben, the first woman doctor in Germany

❋ Elizabeth Garrett Anderson, the first woman doctor in Britain, after whom a famous London women's hospital was named

❋ Golda Meir, first woman Prime Minister of Israel

❋ Indira Gandhi, first woman Prime Minister of India

❋ Margaret Thatcher, first woman Prime Minister of Britain

❋ Vanessa Redgrave, actress and political activist

❋ Nicola Horlick, leading light in the City of London banking world and mother-of-five

❋ Toni Morrison, first African American to win the Nobel Prize for literature

❋ Wilma Mankiller, first woman Chief of the Cherokee Nation

❋ Kids and career ❋

Back in the fifties and earlier, it was relatively easy: dads went out to work and mums stayed home, looking after the kids and being homemakers. (Remember those old ads, with smiling, perfectly groomed mothers in their frilly aprons and high heels? Just how did they do it?)

Then along came the Pill, which gave women greater choice over when – or even whether – to start their families. Economic pressures, too, gradually meant that both parents had to work. Feminism also empowered women, encouraging them to be self-determining and to build their own careers outside of the home. Mums believed they could 'have it all' but it wasn't that simple. Every working mum knows how gut-wrenching it is to have to tear themselves away from a crying toddler as they rush off to work. And, much as they love their kids, stay-at-home mums will admit that conversation with a three-year-old isn't always that stimulating.

It seems mums can't win and being a working mother is a juggling act. It's not perfect, it's not easy, but mums do their best.

> 'At work, you think of the children you have left at home. At home, you think of the work you've left unfinished. Such a struggle is unleashed within yourself. Your heart is rent.'
>
> GOLDA MEIR (1898–1978)

❄ The No. 1 lady detective ❄

Set in Botswana, Alexander McCall Smith's highly successful series of books about the Ladies' No. 1 Detective Agency gives us a wonderful working mother – and a wonderful person – Precious Ramotswe. Mma Ramotswe, as she is usually known, grieves for the death of her baby, born when she was married to no-good musician Note Makote. But she later finds a Good Man – Mr J. L. B. Matekoni – who becomes her second husband. Although they don't have children of their own, the couple adopt two orphans and give them a stable home and family life. Mma Ramotswe spends much of her day drinking bush tea and ruminating on life, morality and the ways of the human race. In a world of uncertainty, her wisdom and sense of what is right is endlessly reassuring. Wouldn't we all like a mother like that?

'All mothers are working mothers.'

AUTHOR UNKNOWN

The artist within

Kids love making things, and getting to work with the scissors, glue and paint is a very special and fun way for mums to spend time with their kids. People always say that childhood goes through in a flash. It's a cliché, I know, but as a mum you'll know just how true it is, and one way to keep those happy memories of your children when they were young is to store away at least one or two of their drawings or homemade greetings cards. Additionally, grandparents and other relatives and friends will be thrilled to receive a homemade greetings card or memento of a trip taken together. So get creative! You are limited only by your imagination ...

❉ Artist's storecupboard ❉

To ensure that there are plenty of raw materials for creating masterpieces (you want to be ready when the Muse strikes), it's a good idea to build up a collection of bits and pieces that may come in handy. Mums and kids can do this together, stashing away their finds in a big cardboard box until required. Don't throw away scraps of wrapping paper – they can make great collages. Pictures from magazines, bits of card, ribbon, tissue paper, sweet wrappers, that beautiful purple foil used to wrap chocolate – all can be pressed into use. Art shops are worth investigating, too: they sell all sorts of wonderful materials that will give that extra oomph to homemade art.

❉ Greetings cards ❉

Commercially produced greetings cards seem to get ever more beautiful and elaborate – and ever more expensive. Making your own cards not only saves money but also produces some wonderful original artwork. Some stationers sell blank cards for you to decorate, or you can make your own from thick paper or thin card – just be sure it's firm enough to stand up on its own.

Snowflake card

Draw a circle on a small piece of white paper and cut it out. Fold it in half, then half again and – if possible – half again. With the paper still folded, cut out shapes along the folds and snip the folded outer edge to create a decorative shape. Open out the paper and you'll have a 'snowflake' with an even geometric pattern radiating out from the centre. Glue the snowflake to coloured card or paper.

Doily card

A similar effect to the snowflake card can be created with less effort by using a very small paper doily – the kind you would put under a glass or cup. Glue it to coloured paper or card to throw the whiteness of the doily into relief.

Stencil card

A similar doily to the one used in the doily card above can be pressed into use again here, this time as a ready-made stencil. You should end up with a beautiful abstract pattern reminiscent of Islamic art, so go for luscious colour combinations – gold with sky blue perhaps, or red with violet. Using Blu-tack or low-tack tape to hold the doily in place on the card or paper, very gently paint over it. Press the brush down onto the doily rather than across it; you want clearly defined shapes, and dragging the brush across the doily will lift the edges of the shapes and allow the paint to seep under. Leave to dry, then carefully remove the doily. Enhance the effect by attaching stick-on 'jewels' (available from stationers and art shops) or other small decorative shapes.

Collage card

Glue cut-out pictures of flowers, fruit, birds – whatever takes your fancy – to card or paper. Wrapping paper often features some pretty motifs to cut out. Decorate your collage card with glitter or glitter glue.

'A child building a sandcastle is not "working hard".
It doesn't seem to him to be a task. It simply fills his
imagination at the time … and anything else is an irritant.'

JONATHAN MILLER (1934–)

🌾 Christmas decorations 🌾

These are fun to make once the colder weather kicks in and
will help mums and kids get in the festive mood – without
that last-minute panic if started well ahead of time. It's a
great rainy-day activity too.

Dough ornaments

Great fun to make, these are sure to adorn the family tree
for years to come. (But remember: they are not edible.)

Mix together 450 g plain flour and 225 g of salt, then
slowly add cold water until you have a smooth dough. Roll
out your dough on a floured surface. Draw your desired
shapes – stars, angels, camels, snowmen, whatever you
fancy – onto a piece of card and cut them out, then lay the
template on your dough and cut around it. Make a hole (big
enough to thread string through) at the top of your
ornaments and then place them on a baking tray and bake in
the oven at the lowest possible setting for at least a couple
of hours, until they are hard but not browned. When the
ornaments are cooled, thread string through the hole for

hanging and use acrylic paints to make them Christmas tree perfect!

Pine cone decorations

Collect some pine cones. Make a hole through the top of each one and insert a loop of wire through the hole. Spray the tips of the cones with gold or silver paint, or fake snow. Thread ribbon through the wire loops and tie the ribbon to the Christmas tree, finishing with a pretty bow.

Card decorations

Cut some suitable shapes from card – reindeer, snowmen, robins, stars, mini-Christmas trees, etc. Make a hole in the top of each shape so you can thread ribbon or string through it and hang it from the Christmas tree. Decorate the shapes with paint and glitter – and don't forget eyes and noses. If you like, add some extra details. A little red ribbon tied around the neck of a snowman would look good, and coloured, stick-on dots could make good buttons.

'To stimulate creativity, one must develop the childlike inclination for play and the childlike desire for recognition.'

ALBERT EINSTEIN (1879–1955)

Paper chains

These are an old favourite but no less enjoyable for that. Cut lots of strips of paper, the same width and length. Vary the paper you use – you could use old wrapping paper, for example, or plain coloured paper. The paper should be firm enough to hold its shape, and all roughly the same weight; if some of the paper is heavier, it could pull the lighter 'links' in the chain out of shape. To make the first link, simply make a loop with a strip of paper and secure the join with adhesive tape. Slot another strip of paper through the first link and secure as before. Continue in this way as long as you like – or as long as the paper holds out. If you are using a selection of different papers, vary the order in which you use them – patterned, then plain, then patterned again, for example.

'Being a mother has made my life complete.'

DARCEY BUSSELL (1969–)

❧ Personalized calendars ❧

A homemade calendar may not have the sophistication of a commercially produced one, but what it lacks in finish it will make up for in charm and originality. You can buy calendars with blank tops for adding your own artwork from stationers and online. Here are some ideas for ways to personalize a homemade calendar:

Birthday calendar

On the blank part of the calendar, stick photos of family members and friends who have birthdays that month. Write the person's name on the appropriate date on the calendar – and perhaps add a smiley face sticker too.

Seasonal calendar

Draw a picture, attach a photograph or create a collage on the blank part of the calendar that reflects the mood of each month. For example, a spring month could show birds and spring flowers; a summer month could feature a beach scene.

Special events calendar

Perfect for remembering special events and achievements as well as being a reminder of important dates throughout the year. Write the event on the relevant date, and decorate it with appropriate stickers – animals, candy shapes, stars, etc. This kind of calendar can be a work-in-progress, for children to add to as important occasions occur.

❄ Keepsake box ❄

A little casket to keep mementoes in – such as baby photos, a lock of baby hair, a first tooth – is something both mums and kids will treasure. Keep an eye out for a suitable item: a small shoebox would do, or any small cardboard box, as long as it's reasonably sturdy. Paint the inside of the box or line it with paper. A couple of layers of tissue paper at the bottom will make a nice cushion for the treasures that the box will hold. Cover the outside of the box with more paper, as fancy as you like, and really go to town on the decorations – the keepsake box should look and feel luxurious. Try stick-on 'jewels' and curls and swirls of glitter pen. To finish, secure the box with a gold ribbon.

✴ Scrapbook ✴

Another old-fashioned idea, but one that has regained popularity in recent years. To really enjoy scrapbooking, neither the kids nor their mums will want to be scrabbling around trying to find pictures, etc, to paste in when that rainy day comes and they fancy a bit of scrapbooking. Again, as with all art, it's much more fun, and more inspiring, to have a wide selection of materials to choose from when the Muse strikes. Cut out pictures from magazines and save them; keep drawings, photographs and any other suitable items; try pressing flowers. Gold and silver stars or other stickers can be used for added decoration. Think of ways to organize the pages – by theme, perhaps, or colour or category – and add personal touches, such as little written notes describing what's on the page, and the date when it was done.

✻ 3-D models ✻

Plasticine is a great material. When I was a kid, I made whole menus from it for my dolls to feast on – Plasticine carrots with green tops, fried eggs, bacon rashers, chops, green peas, tomatoes and bananas were among my culinary creations. Don't knock this humble modelling material – there was a whole garden at the prestigious Chelsea Flower Show in 2009 made from it. It had Plasticine flowers and foliage and even a Plasticine picnic on the lawn. It was a real work of art and was awarded a special prize. Kids can have lots of fun with Plasticine, but for longer-lasting pieces modelling clay is better. This is either self-hardening or needs to be 'cooked' to harden, before painting, according to the manufacturer's instructions.

✻ Silver plaque ✻

For this work of art, you'll need a square or rectangle of strong card, a piece of kitchen foil larger than the card, some strong glue, some black shoe polish, string for hanging the picture and some strong adhesive tape. You'll also need a selection of objects with which to build your picture. Think about what you want it to show and choose materials accordingly. You are going to cover them with the foil, so don't choose anything with too flat a surface that will be obscured by the foil. Corrugated card has a great surface texture that will create that 3-D effect; string, cup hooks, large paper clips work well too.

Assemble your picture, gluing the different items to the card. If you just want to go with an abstract design instead of a picture, that's fine too.

Leave the glue to dry, then lay the foil over the whole thing, gently pressing it into the hollows and grooves around the shapes. Fold the excess foil neatly back behind the card. Using a scrap of cloth, gently work a little of the black shoe polish into the grooves and hollows to 'age' the plaque.

Glue and tape the string to the back and your highly decorative silver plaque is ready to hang.

'Our greatest natural resource is the minds of our children.'

WALT DISNEY (1901–66)

Mothers of the world unite!

When a group of mums come together to achieve a common purpose, they can be a pretty unstoppable force. Mothers' associations come in all shapes and sizes. Often starting small as the brainchild of one or two women, they grow from the grass roots up until, in many cases, they become an inspiring presence on the world stage. Here's to the courage and strength of mothers, the wide world over!

❊ When enough is enough ❊

On 10 August 1976, Anne Maguire was out walking with her four children in Finaghay Road North, in Belfast, Northern Ireland, when an out-of-control car ploughed into them. The driver was wounded IRA gunman Danny Lennon, who was trying to escape the British army patrol that had shot him and were chasing him. Anne's six-week-old baby son Andrew, lying in his pram, was killed instantly, as was her eight-year-old daughter, Anne. The following day, two-and-a-half-year-old John died in hospital. Anne, too, was injured – physically and emotionally (she would later take her own life).

But out of the ashes of this devastating event something extraordinary arose. When Anne's sister, Máiréad Corrigan, made an impassioned plea for peace on television, it struck a chord with the community who had had enough of all the violence and death in their midst and a short while later, the Peace People were born, led by Máiréad and her friend Betty Williams. The two organized a peace march to the graves of the children, which was attended by 10,000 women from both sides of the religious divide. Hundreds wrote letters to them, thousands signed their petitions and marched with them, in Northern Ireland, the Irish Republic and England. The women even set up their own office, to be the centre of their operations. 'The paramilitaries think we are just a funny little movement,' said Betty. 'This is to let them know we mean business.'

In 1976, the movement received the ultimate accolade: Máiréad and Betty, two ordinary Irish women and mothers, were awarded the Nobel Prize for Peace. 'As far as we are concerned, every single death in the last eight years, and every death in every war that was ever fought represents life needlessly wasted, a mother's labour spurned,' said Betty in her acceptance speech.

In 1990, Máiréad received the Catholic Church's prestigious award, the *Pacem in Terris* (Peace on Earth).

> 'If we have no peace, it is because we have forgotten
> that we belong to each other.'
>
> MOTHER TERESA (1910–97)

❋ Unity is strength ❋

Another example of what mothers can achieve is the worldwide organization known as the Mother's Union. Its founder was Mary Sumner, mother-of-three and wife of Anglican cleric, George Henry Sumner. They lived in the parish of Old Arlesford, near Winchester, England.

When, in 1876, her daughter Margaret had her first child, Mary recalled her own sense of inadequacy on becoming a mother. She believed that there was so much more to mothering than just caring for a child's physical needs and that women needed to be properly equipped to do the job. It was time, she decided, to take action. She invited all the mothers of the parish, of all classes, to a meeting in the Rectory. Unfortunately, she was so nervous that she could not put her ideas across, and had to ask the women to reconvene a week later, when she explained the aims of the new society and handed out cards containing practical tips.

The idea took root and from such insignificant beginnings a vast network grew. In 1896, the Central Council of the Mothers' Union was formed, and the organization agreed its own constitution and objectives. Mary Sumner became the Union's first President, and Queen Victoria (mother of nine and later grandmother of forty-two) its first patron.

Today, the Mothers' Union supports mothers and families around the world, with more than 3.6 million members in more than 78 countries. While its underlying message remains a Christian one and its commitment is to marriage and family life, it champions women the world over campaigning to improve their status, hosting literacy programmes, working to reduce child poverty, debt and disadvantage. And all this began in a room in an English rectory back a little over a century ago. Just shows what you can do ...

'Perhaps the greatest social services that can be rendered by anybody to the country and to mankind is to bring up a family.'

GEORGE BERNARD SHAW (1856–1950)

Show that you care

Mums are some of the hardest-working people on the planet but a lot of what they do goes unnoticed because it's just part of the everyday routine of life. How can we show our mums that we appreciate them? Little gifts are lovely to receive, but often it's what we do – rather than what we buy – that really shows we care. It may be corny but it's true: it's the thought that counts.

❀ Gimme a break ❀

It's not glamorous, you can't buy it, it doesn't cost a lot of money – in fact, it's free – but it's a gift most mums would give their eyeteeth for. What is it? A break! Doing something to lighten a mum's load says two things:

A.   You have noticed all the hard work she puts in.
B.   You want to show your gratitude by helping her in return.

Here are some suggestions:

❋ Do the housework for her, while she puts up her feet

❋ Do the ironing

❋ If the mum in question has younger children, babysit one evening (for free!) so she can go out

❋ Run errands for her – for example, collect the dry cleaning, go to the post office, go to the bank, buy Granny's birthday card

❋ Fetch the kids from their friend's house so that Mum can stay in to watch her favourite TV programme

❋ Cook the family supper one night

❋ Do the grocery shopping one week

Little, thoughtful gestures like these register as much, if not more than, expensive presents because they require more effort on the part of the giver than just getting out the cash or the card. The key factor, though, is the spirit in which they are done. They should be offered spontaneously and not done in response to repeated requests – or they won't really be gifts at all.

🌿 What do you do all day? 🌿

Grocery shopping, cooking, washing, housework, ironing, collecting kids from school, being a chauffeur service, remembering birthdays, acting as social secretary for the whole family – the list of what mums do is never-ending.

This is illustrated by a funny story about a husband with a stay-at-home wife. He can't understand how she can be as busy as she says she is – after all, she doesn't have a proper job, does she? 'What do you *do* all day?' he asks her.

The following evening, when the husband comes back from work, he is aghast at what he sees. The floor is littered with toys, dirty dishes cram the sink, the cat is up on the kitchen worktop stealing food, unwashed clothes lie in a pile next to the washing machine, the kids have drawn on the walls with wax crayon and are on the point of murdering each other. In the midst of the carnage is his wife – a picture of serenity as she reclines on the sofa, reading a book and eating chocolates.

'I thought I'd show you what I do all day,' she says.

Point made.

'Cleaning your house while your kids are still growing is like shoveling the walk before it stops snowing.'

PHYLLIS DILLER (1917–)

❋ **Hello, it's me** ❋

So often in our rushed lives we forget to show those we love how much we care for them and value having them in our lives – the very people that matter most to us are often last in the queue for our time and attention. An unexpected little gift, given at times other than birthdays or Christmas, is a simple way to touch Mum's heart and say: 'I think you're great and I love you.' Try giving:

❋ A thank you card

❋ A phone call, text message or email just to say, 'Hello, I'm thinking of you'

❋ A beautiful bunch of flowers

❋ Surprise tickets to the cinema, theatre, concert or exhibition

❋ An invitation to meet for tea or coffee

❋ An apology (if an apology is due)

❋ Some photos that capture special memories – mums love memories

❄ **Weekend treat** ❄

Mums need, and deserve, pampering. How many mums are brought a cup of tea in bed or — outlandish suggestion! — even breakfast in bed? A weekend breakfast in bed is a real treat. How about these delicious dishes to start her day? All are easy to put together, either from simple recipes or ready-made:

❀ Compôte of mixed dried fruit (such as apricots, prunes, pears, apples) and yogurt

❀ Toasted muffins topped with scrambled egg and smoked salmon, with plenty of freshly ground black pepper

❀ Fresh figs with honey and Greek yogurt

❀ Stewed apple, flavoured with cloves and sugar, topped with Greek yogurt or crème fraîche

❀ Beans on granary toast (for extra interest, stir some mixed herbs into the beans while they are heating, and scatter with a little grated cheese)

❀ Sauté potatoes, grilled beef tomatoes and fried bread (for the potatoes, cook the night before, cut into cubes and allow to get cold — then all you have to do in the morning is fry them)

❋ Pancakes or drop scones (homemade or bought) with honey and cottage cheese (if making your own pancakes or scones, save time by preparing the batter the night before and leave it to stand in the fridge overnight; in the morning, beat it lightly to combine the ingredients, then cook as usual)

❋ Warmed waffles (homemade or bought) with maple syrup (available from good supermarkets) or honey

❋ Soufflé mushroom omelette (for this, separate the yolks and whites, beat the whites separately until nearly stiff, then fold into the seasoned and beaten yolks, and cook in the usual way – the omelette will puff up like a soufflé; fill with fried mushrooms in a little crème fraîche, fold over and serve at once for maximum impact)

❋ Luxury fresh salad of fruit and berries (such as pineapple, grapes, papaya, melon, guava, passion fruit, kiwi fruit, strawberries, raspberries, blueberries – mix the colours and sizes for the prettiest effect), followed by a hot, butter-rich croissant

And don't forget the fruit juice, the steaming pot of tea or coffee, and one or two pretty flowers in a small vase on the tray, along with the weekend newspaper. Presentation matters!

❀ A date with indulgence ❀

Because mums are on the go all the time, one thing they rarely get to do is take time out for themselves to relax. Trying to do this at home can be tricky because there are so many chores demanding attention; it's better for a mum to get out of the house, away from her domestic responsibilities, and go on a special 'date' with herself (or with a friend or family member) so that she can indulge in some real relaxation.

One of the most pleasurable ways to relax is to have a massage – and of all the varieties on offer aromatherapy must surely be the most luxurious. Scent has a powerful, primal effect on mood, and the different scented oils work in different ways – some soothe and de-stress, others energize and revive. The aromatherapist will create a mixture suited to the individual's needs. All a mum has to do is surrender to the experience and float off on clouds of fragrance as the therapist gently eases tight muscles and works away all that tension.

If time and budget allow, booking a surprise day, or even weekend, at a health spa is also a wonderful treat for stressed-out mums.

Time out

Mums relish spending quality time with those they love, but finding that time isn't always easy. The way to guarantee it is to arrange a day out, or even a long weekend away somewhere, with Mum as the star guest. For townies, this could be a day out to the coast or country; for country dwellers a day in the city, taking in the shops, lunch and perhaps the theatre in the evening before heading home. Plan it all well in advance – not knowing where to eat or finding that the venue you wanted to visit is closed will ruin the experience.

Lazybones

Remember the mum mentioned earlier who spent the day reading and eating chocolates instead of attending to the chores? Or Mae West in *I'm No Angel* and her famous line: 'Beulah, peel me a grape.' Or Linda Evangelista saying she didn't get out of bed for less than £10,000? OK, so you may not be able to give your mum that kind of money or peel grapes for her, but you can help her liberate her inner couch potato. Here are a few ideas to tempt her.

Couch potato cornucopia

Every proper couch potato needs something to nibble on while slouching on the sofa. This idea is based on the old one of a *cornucopia* – a 'horn of plenty' spilling out goodies.

It requires no cooking, and you can include whatever you fancy (but make sure there's a mixture of savoury and sweet). Simply arrange your ingredients invitingly on a pretty, shallow plate. Here are some suitable tidbits to include:

❋ jelly beans

❋ dates stuffed with marzipan or cream cheese

❋ cubes of cheese

❋ fresh shelled nuts

❋ pieces of crystallized fruit

❋ dried fruits

❋ chocolates (see recipe opposite if you're feeling creative!)

❋ root vegetable chips

❋ mini savoury biscuits

❋ seedless grapes

❋ sugared almonds

❋ marrons glacés

❋ figs

Boozy chocolate truffles

100g (4oz) good-quality plain chocolate
 (70 per cent cocoa solids)
150ml (5fl oz) double cream
1 tablespoon brandy or rum
Cocoa powder, for dusting
Miniature paper cases (optional)
Snuggly sofa, cushion and blanket, to serve

Break the chocolate into chunks and combine with the cream in a small saucepan. Heat gently, stirring, until the chocolate has melted. Pour the mixture into a bowl and leave to cool. Add the brandy or rum and whisk together until paler in colour and fluffy. Transfer to the fridge. When the mixture is firm enough to handle, sprinkle some cocoa powder over a plate and place teaspoonfuls of the mixture on top. Sprinkle with more cocoa, then quickly roll the pieces into balls. Place the truffles in the paper cases or on a paper doily on a pretty plate. Keep refrigerated. Serve, accompanied by a good book or a DVD (see suggestions on page 154).

Sumptuous Smoothie

1 banana
150g raspberries or strawberries
apple juice (optional)
1tsp honey

Slice the banana and blend in a food processor with the raspberries or strawberries. Add some apple juice if you want a runnier consistency. Drizzle with the honey and serve. Healthy *and* gorgeous!

DVDs to snuggle down with

❉ Amelie

❉ Breakfast at Tiffany's

❉ Casablanca

❉ The Devil Wears Prada

❉ High Society

❉ Mamma Mia

❉ Out of Africa

❉ Sense and Sensibility

❉ Sex and the City

❋ Shakespeare in Love

❋ Some Like It Hot

And finally ...

To finish, I'd like to share a personal true story, of one of the most treasured presents I have ever received. It came from my two daughters. It was a Big Birthday for me – one of those with a nought on the end (I won't say which figure appeared before the nought). We'd had the party; we'd had the cake; we'd had the champagne. This was the day after. I had received a formal typed invitation from my two girls, with a venue and time to meet and instructions to keep the day clear, but no information other than that. I duly met them at the appointed place and hour in the centre of London, I discovered that I was going to be taken on a kind of treasure hunt, a magical mystery tour, with enticing clues.

The clues took the form of postcard-sized cards on which my younger daughter had drawn objects that symbolized the different 'treats'. Each card had been placed in a simple brown envelope with a red number written on the front, ranging from 1 to 6. All I had to do was choose an envelope – not necessarily in numerical order – and they would take me to, or give me, whatever that card represented. This was the order I chose:

Card No. 1

My daughters told me I had to start with the envelope showing a '1' on the front. I opened it to find a card inside featuring a floaty cloud. This represented the relaxing aromatherapy massage they had booked for me. I went off to be pummelled and pampered.

Card No. 4

The next card I chose showed a paintbrush. I was so intrigued. It had to be something to do with art. I wondered which of the nearby art galleries we were headed for. I was taken to a well-known venue for a free exhibition they were staging.

Card No. 5

My next choice had a couple of musical notes on the front. We headed back in the direction we had come, towards the Soho area, where the famous Ronnie Scott's jazz club is located. The girls knew that I loved Ronnie's but I knew that they couldn't possibly afford to take me there. I was racking my brains – just where were we going? We ended up in a tiny bar where live blues bands were playing. A fabulous experience.

Card No. 6

This showed a knife and fork. Clearly we were going to eat!
We walked in direction of a sandwich bar. Oh no, I thought,
I don't really want to eat here but I mustn't say anything.
Not to worry. We walked on past and arrived at a pleasant
restaurant just off Trafalgar Square, where we ordered our
meal. There were only two cards left.

Card No. 3

I pulled this out to see a drawing of the world – a round
globe showing the different continents – on the front. Inside
the envelope was another card from a well-known charity,
saying that my daughters had paid for them to plant some
trees in a forest on my behalf. That's where the 'world' came
in – I was helping to save it. I was so moved that I was now
on the point of tears.

Card No. 2

The final clue. All this said on the front was 'daughters'. My
girls then played their trump card. They handed me a
photograph in a frame. It showed my older daughter, at the
age of three, leaning over a hospital cot and stroking the face
of her newborn baby sister. It is my favourite family photo
of all time. Card No. 2. Two daughters. Of course. Was I in
tears? I needed a whole box of tissues.

Perfume, clothes, chocolates and all manner of wonderful gifts – I love them all. But this was so special. Neither of my daughters had much money but they had contrived – with imagination, inventiveness, hard work and perfect planning – to give me a birthday present that I shall never forget. It was a demonstration of love. I still have the envelopes and the cards. I shall treasure them to my dying day.